THE EMOTIONAL ALCHEMY OF HEALING

FINDING A WAY FORWARD WHEN LIFE CHANGES

RACHEL MARIE RABATIN

CONTENTS

To those who have challenged me and to those who have held me up: Thank you for your support and tremendous love. I hope you find the gold that speaks to you within these pages. Be well on your journey; may you find all the joy the world has to offer.

INTRODUCTION

> *"Knowing yourself is the beginning of all wisdom."*
>
> — ARISTOTLE

I'm not the same person I was when I wrote my first book… except that I am. I'm the same me I've always been, yet I've reached a new stage in my journey. In the introduction to that book, I wrote about a shared home filled with love, laughter, and dreams for the future. That was true for me then, but my dreams have changed, and that home is now a memory kept on the shelf. The me I am now has a new chapter in her story to tell… and it's one I believe may help you.

As we all are, I'm on a continuous voyage into healing and growth, and the words you're reading now serve as a follow-up to *An Original Grief Guide*. I've learned more about myself since writing it, and that learning curve began during the process of its creation. I'm further along the pathway of healing, and my eyes have been opened. Everything I had planned is gone, my dreams have changed, and I'm looking at the world through new eyes.

Looking back, I can tell you that I knew some things, but I also knew nothing. I believed I was in a good place, and to an extent, that was true. But every one of us still has learning to do, and I'm no exception. I mentioned in my first book that I believe I'm meant to be of service, and just like healing, that isn't a once-and-done job. For as long as I have breath left in me, I want to use it to connect and help others, and through doing so, I continue to learn more about myself. As I understand more about the process of healing, the drive to share my experiences only grows.

Life's going to come at you, and you've got to grow with it. For me, that came with enormous change. I discovered that what I thought I wanted wasn't what was going to bring me real peace and happiness, and I was forced to change course in order to stay true to myself. My story is one of getting back to basics, and the healing that's coming to me through that is huge … But I've got to be honest with you: so is the pain that comes alongside it.

You'll have come across Elizabeth Kübler-Ross's model of grief: the five stages that we move through when we're grieving. I've written about how this model is limited in the way it's so commonly cited, as the process we move through to reach closure, and Kübler-Ross has said this herself. In a conversation with leading mental health expert Dr. Ken Druck, she explained that the stages were always intended to be guideposts, not a precise roadmap toward closure. We can't pack our emotions away into sealed boxes and expect to put them away forever—and trying to do so will only set us up for a painful wake-up call. Healing is an ongoing journey. To heal a wound properly, you need to change the dressing. You can't expect to bandage it once and be done any more than you can expect to move through five clear-cut stages of grief. Healing is messy, and moving through it doesn't follow a direct route. You have to keep an eye on that dressing all the time.

There's a phrase I like to use to describe the process I've been going through over the last couple of years, and this book is all about sharing that journey and the strategies I've been using with you. That phrase is "emotional alchemy," and I'm so excited to introduce you to it... because the liberation it can bring you is immense.

The idea behind emotional alchemy is that it's possible to take your pain and turn it into great strength and power—tools you can use to find your inner peace and live your most authentic life.

Whether you've lost a loved one, you've left behind an important relationship, been through a significant life change, or news about your health has reframed your experience of life, you're on a journey of healing—one that's lined with painful reminders, triggers, and emotional struggles. I know. I'm on one, too. It's a journey that continues long after the catalyst event, one that still stretches ahead of you when you've finished grief counseling and you feel like you should already have learned every trick in the book. You're a changed person, but you're still in pain, and the changes that come with healing are tough to handle. Perhaps there are relationships in your life that no longer bring you peace, and the thoughts and emotions that come with that can be terrifying. You know that something needs to shift ... and that's why you're here.

I can't promise you instant shortcuts or some magical cure to the pain ... But I can tell you that there's something better ahead, and I can share with you the art of becoming an emotional alchemist. But let me be frank: it's not going to be easy. You're going to have to get uncomfortable to get comfortable. You'll have to allow yourself to feel your pain in order to feel the peace on the other side. By embracing every emotion, you can use that fuel and learn to fly.

Your journey begins as soon as you turn this page ...

1

THE GOAL LINE MOVES: YOU DON'T KNOW UNTIL YOU KNOW

"When everything seems to be going against you, remember that an airplane takes off against the wind, not with it."

— HENRY FORD

It took me moving from Ohio to Arizona to learn the truth about Native American culture, but it took me coming back home two decades later to understand what had truly been taken from them. Their communities have suffered staggering loss, yet there are tales of renewal, rediscovery, and hope amidst the pain. This is something common to every story of loss, and it's something I see reflected in my own healing journey.

As someone who lives their life with gratitude as a starting point, Thanksgiving has always been a time for me, as it is for many Americans, to get together with people I love and express my gratitude for what I have. But now that I know more about the truth behind the story, it has also become a time for me to reflect, to remind myself that what we think is happening isn't always what is. And there's solace in this as I think about my own healing journey and the changes I've been through since I wrote *An Original Grief Guide*.

This last year has been a journey of coming home, of getting back to my roots. Everything around me was shaking, and everything I thought I knew was shifting under my feet. I needed something to make me feel steady.

My choice to leave Arizona, a place I had made my home for two decades, was inspired when I visited my friend Martha. I was seeing signs of her everywhere—a conversation with someone about her name, a character in a TV show, a Tom Waits song on Spotify… When I looked her up to check on her, I discovered that not only was she sick, but she was in the hospital just three miles away from me. I made a plan to visit her and take her breakfast, but my morning didn't go to plan. I was late, and I was mad at myself for not making it there when I said I would. But, as it turned out, I arrived at the perfect time. Martha's husband wasn't available to pick her up from the hospital, and she needed a ride home—a ride I could provide. It might not have been the time I wanted to get there, but it was perfect timing for my friend and what she needed at that moment. I gave her a ride home, and on the way from her house to mine, I reflected on how good it felt to be there for her, the realization slowly dawning that I had a life full of Marthas—people who I wanted to show up for. I had family members at home who could use support, and it struck me with astounding clarity that I had to be there for them. I wasn't where I needed to be.

Leaving the desert and the life I'd made there was my own choice, but that doesn't mean it was easy. In fact, it was extremely painful. It still is. I had to be willing to let go. In my first book, I wrote that I was married and building my dream home. I'm no longer married. That home was built, and I lived there for a short time… but now that house has been sold, and I'm in a different place. Everything I said about my happiness in my first book was true at the time that I wrote it, and it was an important part of my journey of healing and growth. But there were a lot of big stressors in my life at that time, too—things I perhaps wasn't recognizing yet—and as I learned more about what I needed to find my peace, I understood that I had to shed tools and lifestyles that had once been part of my healing process. They *were* part of my healing process, but healing is just that—it's a process. What helps you to heal one year may not be what helps you the next. Once you think you know the rules, they change again. I discovered that I was living my life on autopilot. I had become automatic, working crazy hard toward a dream that I was in danger of losing sight of the more I devoted myself to working. I realized that if I was to truly reach that dream, I had to take a different approach. I had to be fully present within myself and start making choices for me—no matter how hard they were.

I'm not the only person I know who's experienced this pull to get back to my roots. It's a common story among my friends, and there are plenty of sound reasons why we might do it. Our roots are the foundation from which we grow, the thing that anchors us when life gets tough. We spend our lives trying out new things and new places, but when something doesn't fit, many of us experience a pull to get back to our origins, to understand where our journey started and remind ourselves of who we are underneath the scars left by everything that's happened to us. Our roots have an impact on our past, present, and future: they show us where we came from and help us to understand how we developed into the person we see before us in the mirror; they help us to see what's important to us; they show us which path we need to take in order to prevent ourselves from repeating past mistakes.

Whatever the outcome may be, going back to where we came from is grounding, and it paves the way for understanding. We uncover more about our background and where our values developed, and we understand more about the people who raised us and their beliefs and attitudes. It also helps with the healing process—and in my case, when going home brought as much pain as leaving Arizona did, I've seen that to be true. We can't heal pain we're unable to acknowledge or pain that we've buried. Going home forces us to face it and open ourselves up to healing.

Returning to where we came from gives us a chance to mend broken bridges that have led to emotional separation over the years—and when that isn't possible, it allows us to take the steps we need to move on. We find ourselves revisiting familiar memories, reuniting with old friends, and remembering the value of long-lasting connections and the perspective of those who've known us the longest. Many of us leave home in the first place to escape from something, but no matter where we go, we are the common denominator in all our circumstances. That's something we'll never escape from, and when we're forced to face that, we're offered an opportunity to learn about ourselves and grow into the person we were always meant to become. With that often comes an inspiration to fight through the challenges we face, driven by the realization that those who came before us had to do exactly that in order to live a life they believed in. We are reminded of who we are and who we want to be.

Just as it is important for the Native Americans and anyone who wants that link to their roots, it has been important to me to be reminded of my history. But going home taught me that when you've been gone for a long time, people get used to you being away. The support you imagine might be there waiting for you when you return may not be, and the help you offer your loved ones may not be welcomed; it may even be seen as interference instead of the love it was intended to show. In my head, I was going home, but the reality I experienced was that I was going back to a place that *used* to be my home. It was important for me to return to my roots, and I'm grateful to have spent the time with the people I still have there, but the healing I've gained from going through that process wasn't the healing I expected, and I found myself having to heal from things I hadn't been able to acknowledge needed my attention until I put myself on the ground.

It was a turning point, and it's one many of us have to experience, whether it's in the form of a homecoming or the realization that a dream we have can't be realized. We can see a similar narrative playing out in the business world, which lives in the shadow of the American Dream. The number of hopeful business owners whose dreams of success are shattered within the first few years reflects exactly that turning point for many people. The failure rate of startups within the first few years of business is thought to stand at between 30% and 50%. People put everything into their businesses, and if they fail, they're faced with incredible loss. I have a friend dealing with this now. He's struggling to keep his business afloat—a business that's part of his identity. If he doesn't make it, he will be faced with feelings of loss and existential questions about who he is.

We'll all be faced with a turning point like this at some time. Whatever the nature of our loss, we will always experience pain. That's a given. What matters is what we do with it and how we move ourselves forward and grow from our experiences.

Over the coming chapters, we're going to look at a tool used in Dialectical Behavioral Therapy (DBT) known as "radical acceptance," but I want us to begin working with it before we get there. I had to make some difficult decisions to get me on the path I knew I needed to take, and part of doing that involved questioning my thinking and looking at whether I was leaning into a forced narrative or aligning with my true self. That meant looking at both positive and negative possible outcomes rather than focusing only on the negative ones and allowing fear to stop me from following my path. Doing this helps to get your thinking onto a middle ground, removing your biases and allowing you to move forward authentically.

➤ Tricks for Your Emotional Alchemy Bag

Consider a challenge you need to face, and make a list of both the potential positive and negative outcomes. In DBT, this is known as tackling the "What If?" Bias. Here's an example addressing the fear of going to a party to get you started.

What if the outcome is negative?	What if the outcome is positive?
What if I get overwhelmed by seeing so many people at once?	What if I see someone I haven't seen in a long time?

In the next chapter, we're going to take a closer look at the issues that arise when you make those difficult changes, whether they're ones you've chosen or ones that have been forced onto you. It's not easy, but the amazing thing about being human is that we're just like our muscles: we have to break down a little in order to get stronger.

2

ALWAYS LOVE: MOVING FORWARD WITH GOOD VIBES

"True forgiveness is when you can say, 'Thank you for that experience.'"

— OPRAH WINFREY

When we talk about grief, we're often talking about the process of dealing with the death of a loved one. This is a process I'm all too familiar with, and it's been a big part of my healing journey. This last year, though, I've been working through a different kind of grief. My life has been touched less by death than it has in other difficult periods, yet I've lost people… and the complication in that for me is that some of those are losses I've chosen. I've lost a number of relationships, and that has involved grieving on multiple levels—grieving for what has been lost and grieving for what I thought those relationships were.

Sometimes, when we walk away from a relationship, be it a friendship, a romantic relationship, or a familial relationship, it isn't necessarily anyone's fault—it's simply that we aren't good for each other. Sometimes, someone *is* at fault, but that doesn't mean you can't come from a place of love when you're dealing with the situation.

CUTTING TIES

Walking away from a relationship is never easy, but there are times when we have to acknowledge that keeping someone in our lives isn't good for us. This can be a very difficult call to make, and if you're considering it, you're going to be dealing with feelings of guilt and regret. To make it easier to see past these heavy feelings that cloud the decision-making process, consider the following points, and think about whether they apply to the relationship you're thinking of ending.

- There's no give and take, and you find yourself in a position where you're constantly being taken from; or every time that person does something for you, it comes with strings attached, and you're expected to do something in return.
- The other person fails to take responsibility for their actions or apologize when they've made a mistake. Perhaps they instead lean into the victim role, or maybe they simply like being right. Either way, this isn't a healthy situation for you to be in.

- They attempt to control you. There could be good psychological reasons for this, and it may be that it results from a lack of control in their own life, but that doesn't mean it's good for you. If someone is constantly telling you what to do or say, you may be better off walking away from them.
- Your boundaries aren't being respected. Once you've laid down a boundary, you have a right to expect it to be honored. If someone is constantly violating your boundaries, you owe it to yourself to take a step back from that relationship.
- The other person often makes out that they're being oppressed or wronged, either by blaming you for things that aren't your responsibility or coming up with excuses for their unfair behavior.
- They're frequently judgmental or put you down a lot, looking for imperfections or weaknesses in you that will make you feel small. You may feel like you're walking on eggshells for fear of being criticized.
- They're dishonest, and you catch them frequently lying to you or skimming the edges of the truth.
- They're manipulative and will stop at nothing to get their own way. You may find yourself getting trapped in mind games or being gossiped about. This isn't okay, and you don't have to live with a relationship like this.

- Their needs seem to always come above (or even at the expense of) yours. They may be self-obsessed and show little regard for what you need.

Making calls to move away from relationships is something I've been through in multiple areas of my life recently, and that's an inevitable part of growing and changing. It's hard, and it's painful, but that doesn't mean it's not right. There are points in life where we have to take stock and make conscious decisions about where we are versus where we want to be and what we want from life. Making those changes isn't possible if we carry on with everything we're currently doing. We have to take away the things—or the people—that no longer fit with our path. Relationships change. That's a part of life. There's a point at which you have to choose yourself. You have to be able to stand up for what you need and recognize when that isn't being honored. That can be very hard—sometimes, when we're trying to be kind and loving, what happens is that we put our own needs after someone else's—sometimes to the point that we lose sight of what our own needs are. But you can still let go of those relationships and come from a place of love—even when you're the one making that choice.

Sometimes, we simply outgrow relationships. There are multiple reasons this can happen. It may be that the only thing linking the two of you is the past, and as you grow and develop as a person, you may find that your views and interests no longer align. Perhaps you find that the only things you have to talk about are shared memories, which in itself isn't a bad thing, but if it's the only thing linking you with someone, growing both together and individually becomes difficult. Regardless of whether there's a lot of shared history or not, you may find that you don't have much in common anymore.

Significant life changes like new jobs or home towns can make you grow in separate directions, and you may feel like the other person is locked into a particular phase of life while you move ahead in a different direction at great speed. This is often the case for people who are interested in continually working on themselves and pushing themselves toward their dreams—if someone in your life doesn't have the same growth mindset that you do, it can be challenging to maintain the relationship. The other issue here is that people will always see you in a certain way, and no matter how much you've grown and changed, their expectation of how you will think or react remains static. In some cases, it doesn't matter how you really react—what they'll see is what they expect, and this can leave you feeling confused and misunderstood.

Another thing that can happen is that you notice a change in yourself when you're with a particular person. Perhaps the connection is beginning to feel forced, and you find yourself reverting to a younger version of yourself to make it feel less awkward. The result of this is a gap between who you are when you're not with them and the old character traits that come out when you're in their company. This can feel very tiring because you're essentially reverting to a person you no longer embody in order to keep that relationship alive, and you may even find yourself having to feign interest in things that no longer have relevance to your life. This can be enough of a problem on its own, but it becomes particularly problematic if you end up falling back into bad habits or moving away from the good habits you've been trying to cultivate in order to propel yourself toward your goals. A good example of this is when you're trying to keep yourself in a positive mindset, and one of your friends is constantly complaining about work. Engaging with the old habit may be uncomfortable for you, and it affects your ability to work on your new mindset. No one's to blame, but you're both operating on different levels, and moving away from that relationship may be better for both of you.

Sometimes, a relationship can leave us feeling stressed out or exhausted. It's always important to consider how you feel in someone else's presence. If you find yourself dreading seeing them or finding ways to avoid spending one-on-one time with them, or if you come away feeling tired or stressed at the end of your encounter, that's a red flag marking that they may not be good for you anymore. A positive relationship is inspiring and energizing; if you're feeling the opposite of this, continuing to force it isn't fair to either of you.

Finally, if you feel like you're the one making all the effort (or if you're aware that the other person is doing this), it's worth considering whether that relationship is balanced. In a healthy, positive relationship, you want to spend your time with the other person; if you feel obligated, that's a sign that the relationship is no longer right for you.

MOVING AWAY FROM A RELATIONSHIP

It's one thing to recognize that you've outgrown a relationship; it's quite another to walk away from it or make the changes needed to bring it back to a healthy place—and to do so lovingly. If you're struggling with this, try one of these action steps (and if you don't notice a change, try another).

- **Talk to the other person; find out where they stand and how they feel about your relationship.** This is a chance for you to let them know how you're feeling and hash out any misunderstandings, and it may be an opportunity for the two of you to redefine your relationship and move forward in a new direction.
- **Take a break from the relationship to give yourself a greater perspective.** This can be as simple as saying, "Let's catch up in a couple of weeks." It doesn't necessarily require you to tell the other person that you're consciously taking a

break from them, although, of course, this is an option too.

- **Stop forcing the relationship if it's costing you a lot of time and energy.** This is particularly applicable to those relationships where you feel like you're always the one making the effort to reach out to them and make plans to connect. If that feels like an uphill battle every time, there's no reason you have to keep putting yourself through the wringer. Simply pulling back on making that effort may be the best thing for both of you.

- **Back off gradually.** If a relationship is fading and there's no solid problem to address, a big talk is probably not what either of you needs. Try reaching out less frequently and engaging less often. If the relationship has run its course but there's no animosity, this may be the best approach.

- **Express your need to walk away from the relationship.** This can be a difficult one, and you'll need to weigh the cost carefully, but in some circumstances (for example, if you're trying to heal and your relationship triggers this trauma), communicating your needs will make it clear to the other person why you're making the decision.

- **Let go of your guilt.** Remind yourself that outgrowing friendships and other relationships is a normal part of life, and try to view the process as a natural evolution. I realize this is easier said than done, and I've had to work through a lot of guilt as I've gone through various changes in my life recently. Here are a few strategies I've found helpful in letting go of that guilt:

- **Rather than trying to ignore how you're feeling, name it.** Addressing guilt effectively requires us to accept how we're feeling and sit with that with as little judgment as possible so we can understand the intricacies of why we're feeling the way we are.
- **Think about where your guilt is coming from.** Noticing when we're blaming ourselves for things that aren't our fault is as important as taking responsibility for our mistakes. It's common to feel guilty about severing ties with someone who loves us, but it's important to recognize that there's nothing wrong with doing so. We have to be able to honor ourselves, and as long as we act with kindness and love, it's okay to walk away from a relationship that's no longer good for us.
- **Take the lessons forward.** I know how all-consuming guilt can be when it's combined with the sadness of losing someone, and I've learned that before you can leave it behind, you have to accept it. Tough as that is, it does offer a payoff: What can you learn from it? How can you prevent a similar situation from happening in the future? Think

about what you'd do differently within that relationship if you were to start again, and think about the triggers that prompted your decision to leave it. These are all useful lessons that will help you navigate future relationships.

○ **Practice gratitude.** This is a big one for me. If I find myself falling into that all-consuming feeling of guilt and self-doubt, I try to bring myself back to gratitude. I'm thankful for my strength and clarity, for my commitment to honoring my needs, for my ability to remain loving even when it's not what I'm seeing given back, and I'm thankful for the peace that walking away from that relationship has given me.

○ **Practice self-compassion rather than negative self-talk.** We'll look at this more closely in Chapter Four, but it's an important tool in letting go of guilt, which in itself can trigger heavy self-criticism. Ask yourself what you would say to a friend in the same situation. You probably wouldn't be anywhere near as harsh as you're being to yourself. In fact, you'd probably remind them of their strengths and why making this decision is the right thing for them, and you deserve to give that same kindness to yourself.

○ **Recognize your guilt as an alarm call that tells you what areas of yourself you might want to work on.** For example, if you're feeling guilty about the way you handled a particular interaction, you can use that to shape how you approach a similar situation in the future. Similarly, you can recognize what your guilt is telling you about your character. If you're feeling guilty about hurting the other person, that shows that you have empathy and didn't act with bad intentions, and this may help you let go of that guilt.

○ **Forgive yourself for your mistakes.** You're human. We're meant to make mistakes—it's how we grow and become better. That mistake shouldn't define you; it's simply a tool you can work with to move forward.

○ **Talk through your feelings with someone you trust.** Guilt isn't always an easy emotion to talk about, and that can make you feel very isolated, in turn making healing more difficult. Sharing our feelings helps us to release tension and gain more perspective.

Recognizing that I can put myself first and still come from a place of love has been huge for me. It's what has allowed me to make the changes I needed to make in order to move forward on my own journey. Gratitude has always been an important baseline, and whenever I flail, I come back to it. This has been helpful to me as I've worked through these changes. I'm thankful to the people who pushed my boundaries because they taught me how to be strong, how to fend for myself, and how to be a better me. I'm thankful that this is a tool I already have in my toolkit.

Grief can mess with your operating system, and this is why we see bad things happening as a result. It's why we see angry divorces filled with hate and revenge—but it doesn't have to be that way.

FEELING YOUR EMOTIONS

Grief can make people do crazy things. Losing what we know or what we thought life was going to be can fuck us up—so much so that people do heinous things that are outside of their moral code, often as a result of avoiding the truth. Repressing our emotions is dangerous. The emotions don't disappear just because we bury them— they just come out in other ways. In fact, studies have shown that people who frequently repress their emotions often pay more attention to their physical health and end up looking for physical solutions for emotional issues. Just as we must treat a wound to prevent infection, we must treat our emotional health to prevent mental health problems like stress, depression, and anxiety.

The problem is that it's not always easy to tell when you're repressing your emotions. I know I've had unhealthy coping mechanisms in the past, and it's only with hindsight that I've been able to see what was really going on for me there. I've learned from those mistakes, and I'm much better at seeing the signs now. Actively seeking to feel your most difficult emotions is painful, let me tell you, but it's the only way to process them and come out the other side stronger, and the clarity it gives you is what allows you to move forward with love and leave those relationships in the kindest way you can. For me, a future filled with peace and mental fortitude is a far greater prize than a future in which those things are inaccessible, no matter what I have to go through to get there.

Key to recognizing whether you're in danger of repressing your emotions is being able to reflect on your thoughts and behaviors. If you believe that feeling negative emotions makes you weak or you're embarrassed by them, you're far more likely to push them down. Similarly, if you believe that you're categorically fine and never have to deal with negative emotions, that's telling you that there's probably something you're burying from yourself. To be human is to feel negative emotions from time to time … If you never do, that's a sign that you need to address your thinking and look at what's really going on there. If you're actively pushing down your emotions or distracting yourself from feeling them through escaping behaviors like video gaming, binge-watching Netflix, or turning to alcohol or drugs, that's also telling you that you have emotions to deal with. If you don't, the result may be an eruption of built-up emotions and difficulty with recognizing the things in your life that are causing you harm. You can also look at your reactions to other people as a signpost for whether there's something you need to address. If you don't like being asked how you feel or you often put on a positive face in public to avoid talking about your feelings, you probably have some difficult emotions bubbling under the surface that you're subconsciously trying to avoid. The same may be true if you struggle in situations where other people are being emotional or expressing difficult feelings. If you notice that you're always trying to move the conversation around to more positive topics, it's worth asking yourself why that is.

Coping With Difficult Emotions

Let's be real: Allowing yourself to feel those painful emotions isn't fun. That's why most of us try to escape them, at least some of the time. But as someone who's tried both approaches, I can tell you that finding ways to cope with your feelings without ignoring them is far more healing than the alternative. The best starting point is to try to understand your relationship with your emotions. Your attitude to negative emotions will affect how you respond to them, and it may have become a habit to push them away. The only way to break that habit is to notice when it's happening, and that starts with recognizing your attitude to them. It's also helpful to think about the purpose of human emotions. Every single one of them serves us in some way, no matter how painful, and remembering this helps us let go of the idea that they're threatening. Emotions serve an evolutionary function, guiding us toward behaviors that will improve our chances of survival and help us develop. Let's take the seven basic emotions as an example of this. Each one serves a distinct purpose:

- **Joy:** Reminds us of what's truly important
- **Surprise:** Allows us to focus on new circumstances or situations
- **Anticipation:** Helps us to plan and look toward the future
- **Anger:** Enables us to fight problems as they arise
- **Fear:** Protects us from dangerous situations
- **Disgust:** Helps us to reject things that are harmful or unhealthy
- **Sadness:** Connects us with the people we love

Negative emotions also provide a useful counterpoint to positive emotions. We need the bad feelings in order to get the most out of the good ones, and you can't have one without the other.

The next step is to get to know how your emotions affect your body. There is a personal variation here: for me, for example, anxiety shows up as a racing feeling. I feel like I'm going fast, and I have to stop and breathe through it in order to address what's making me feel anxious. For other people, anxiety manifests as a tightness in the chest or a headache. Pay attention to the sensations in your body when you're feeling a particular emotion so that you become familiar with the patterns and recognize what's going on. It's also helpful to work out what triggers your emotions; that will help you to prepare for their potential appearance and manage them more effectively. I know that rushing myself triggers my anxiety, for example, so I always allow time around engagements to take the time I need to get there at a pace that's comfortable for me.

The next step is a tricky one. Coping with difficult emotions means learning how to live with them. Your emotions will push back if you try to push them away, so you have to invite them in and accept that they're going to be your guests for a while. Acknowledging them makes this easier. I think the easiest way to do this is to name them, aiming not to beat yourself up for experiencing them. Remember that acknowledging an emotion won't make it any worse and that you won't feel like this forever. Then you have to sit with that emotion, by which I mean paying attention to it when it shows up and considering the sensations it prompts in your body. To take the example of anxiety again: for me, it's noticing the feeling of my body going fast that tells me I need to slow down and feel the emotion that's causing it. I'm not trying to change or fix that emotion; I'm trying to manage it so it doesn't overwhelm me, and I can move through it. Ask yourself what that emotion is telling you. Think about what triggered it and what it's trying to communicate. Does it tell you what you need right now? For me, that feeling of anxiety is often telling me that I need to slow down and take care of myself, and I try to honor that as much as I can. That's the best way I can stop it from escalating, and if I can do that, I'm better in every area of life. Taking a moment to think about what triggered your emotion and what it's telling you will help you avoid acting impulsively and instead act in a way that will be helpful to you. That action will vary according to the emotion and the circumstances in which it arises. It might involve problem-solving or taking some time out to take care of yourself; it might be managed best through breathing exercises or engaging mindfully in a practical activity like exercising or cooking.

As you become more adept at managing your more difficult emotions, your emotional literacy will develop, and this will make you not only more sensitive to your own emotions but also better able to understand those of the people around you. This can be very empowering, and doing this for myself has certainly given me a greater sense of control and understanding.

Processing our emotions is important in order to keep us on track and prevent us from doing things that defy our moral compass or harm our wellbeing. There are countless terribly sad stories about people straying from their path, and I think facing our emotions and riding out the storms they bring with them is key to helping us avoid this.

➤ Tricks for Your Emotional Alchemy Bag

Practice noticing and naming your emotions. The next time you notice a change in how you're feeling, take a moment to name the emotion that's affecting you. Imagine looking out the window at a bird feeder. As you may name the different breeds of birds that visit, you can practice observing and naming the emotions that come to you. This will bring you a greater sense of clarity about what you're feeling, and observing yourself from a distance as you would a bird feeder will help you pay attention to your experience without applying judgment or beating yourself up for what you're experiencing.

Emotional healing is vital if we're to process our grief in a healthy way and grow from it. It's important to be able to let go of those past hurts and avoid falling into blame and hate if we're to move forward and become the best version of ourselves, treating those we leave behind with kindness in spite of how we may feel. And to do that requires becoming an emotional alchemist …

3

FROM PAIN TO JOY: BECOMING THE EMOTIONAL ALCHEMIST

"Crying does not indicate that you are weak. Since birth, it has always been a sign that you are alive."

— CHARLOTTE BRONTË

I cry a lot. I always have, and I know it's good for me. But this isn't something I've always been comfortable with. It makes people uneasy, and they don't always know how to deal with it. There have been times that I've questioned why I'm feeling the way I am or whether I'm feeling too much. I'd wonder what was wrong with me or ask myself if crying so much was stopping me from healing. But the reality is that it was always something that was helping me to heal. This is now something I've come to understand, and I'm grateful for my ability to let my emotions flow out of me so that I can address what they're asking me to listen to.

CRYING IT OUT

Philosophers as far back in history as Ancient Greek and Roman times hypothesized that tears work to purify us, allowing us to release stress and emotional pain. There are three distinct categories of tears: continuous tears, reflex tears, and emotional tears. It is this third category that is thought to be of most value to our health, flushing out toxins like stress hormones, while the first two, which function to keep our eyes clean and protected, are 98% water. The act of crying allows us to release endorphins, which help to ease pain (both emotional and physical).

> *"Most people think we cry because we're sad. And that can be true. But crying is connected to our central nervous system and our body's natural impulse to self-regulate"*
>
> — @THE.HOLISTIC.PSYCHOLOGIST

Crying has a soothing effect, allowing us to regulate our emotions and reduce distress, activating the parasympathetic nervous system and allowing us to relax. With the feel-good hormones that are released in the process, emotional pain is released in much the same way that swearing when we hurt ourselves allows us to increase our resilience to physical pain. It helps us to feel better in the moment that we engage in it, and the calming effect it creates helps us to sleep more easily when we're struggling with difficult emotions. Because it's an attachment behavior, it also helps us to get support from those around us.

RADICAL ACCEPTANCE

Radical acceptance is a term I only came across relatively recently, but in researching it, I realized that it's something I've been working on actively as part of my healing journey. Becoming comfortable with letting those tears flow and allowing myself to feel the emotions behind them was part of that. The idea of radical acceptance comes from Buddhist teachings, but the term was coined in 1993 by Marsha Linehan, the founder of Dialectical Behavioral Therapy (DBT). It refers to the practice of consciously acknowledging and honoring difficult emotions and circumstances, accepting the situation as it is rather than ignoring it or wishing it were something else. This allows us to regulate our emotions and recognize what truly matters to us while moving away from unhelpful thought patterns. Radical acceptance doesn't mean that we approve of the situation or that we're giving up on trying to improve it. It means facing up to what's happening and confronting those difficult emotions head-on. We explored the importance of feeling your emotions in Chapter Two, and this is a part of radical acceptance.

Marsha Linehan outlined a 10-step plan for practicing radical acceptance:

1. Observe that you're fighting reality ("This isn't what was meant to happen").
2. Remind yourself that the situation is as it is and what happened can't be changed.
3. Remind yourself that there are reasons why the situation is as it is.
4. Use your whole being (body, mind, and spirit) to practice accepting the situation. You might use relaxation techniques, positive self-talk, visualization, and mindfulness.
5. Note all the behaviors you'll engage in if you can accept the fact of the situation, and begin practicing those behaviors as if you've already come to a place of acceptance.
6. Visualize yourself believing the things you don't want to accept, and note what you'll do when you accept the things that right now seem impossible to be okay with.
7. Pay attention to the sensations in your body when you're thinking about the situation you need to accept.
8. Allow difficult feelings like grief, sadness, and disappointment to surface.
9. Acknowledge that life is still worth living, even when you're in pain.

10. If you find that you're resistant to practicing radical acceptance, list the pros and cons of the situation.

Accepting my tears and allowing myself to experience the emotions that came with them was a big part of the process for me, a process I'd begun long before I learned about radical acceptance. When I hold in what I'm not supposed to, I could erupt with the weight of it. I have to let it flow out of me and be grateful: what's flowing out of me is what I need to deal with. As the ancient philosophers knew, I'm purifying myself by allowing myself to release what's going on inside me.

THE RIGHT SUPPORT

Being who you are unashamedly? Fuck yeah! But that does require you to have the right support. It means surrounding yourself with like-minded people who understand you and love you as you are—and as I've let go of some of those relationships that weren't supporting me as I needed, I've had the room to let new ones in—ones that allow me to be fully me and which give me the confidence to be myself and be open and unapologetic about my experience.

A big part of making this transition was being honest with myself about my experience in different situations and with different people. If you had asked me if I had the right people around me before I began that process, I would have said yes, and that was my truth at the time. But sometimes, we must ask ourselves difficult questions if we're going to avoid keeping ourselves back from the growth and healing we truly need. If you're struggling with this at the moment, I'd encourage you to ask yourself these four questions:

1. What's my experience of being around this person?
2. How am I reacting to them physically?
3. Do I feel accepted and loved however I show up?
4. Am I being listened to, and when I ask for what I need, is that request being honored?

I found slowing down and asking myself these questions hugely helpful to recognizing those relationships that were no longer good for me. Paying attention to my physical reactions was particularly important. If I notice my anxiety triggers bubbling and my stress rising when I'm with a particular person, that speaks volumes about how much good that relationship is really doing me.

THE POWER OF SELF-CARE

Self-care has been an important part of my journey, allowing me to feel those difficult emotions, assess the relationships that were troubling me, and take care of myself both physically and emotionally within that.

When I first moved back home, I underwent a series of ketamine treatments supervised by a nurse practitioner. Ketamine therapy is a treatment in which low doses of ketamine are administered to address a variety of mental health conditions, including anxiety, depression, and PTSD. The treatment involves an intense experience that triggers a change in insight, understanding, and behavior and often has antidepressant effects, which many patients have said has helped to improve their symptoms within hours of treatment.

My treatments weren't easy experiences, and each one took me some time to recover from, but they taught me some important lessons about feeling my emotions and keeping myself safe within them. During one particularly valuable session, I watched scenes and emotions play out around me while I stayed safe in the middle. I conceptualized this as "staying in the pocket," watching the scenes play out around me but also feeling it all. The things I was watching were things that had happened and that I was dealing with: they were part of my story, and I was okay to look at them and feel them. Getting to that point was a gradual process, and it doesn't mean that feeling them was easy. But I knew I was okay, and I felt safe enough to look at them and ride the wave. Staying in the pocket was something I took forward with me and can still get myself back to when I'm experiencing difficult emotions. It also showed me, by giving me specific slots to work with those emotions in a safe space, that I have the power to design my life to incorporate those spaces. This is self-care.

What Self-Care Has Looked Like for Me

I'm currently working on making self-care a solid part of my routine, and what I'm finding is that the routine is as important as the self-care itself. This makes sense—medical professionals note the health benefits of having a routine, citing an increased ability to manage stress and improved sleep and lifestyle choices. I personally thrive in routine, and there's less need for decision-making in the moment. The decision is already made; I'm simply following through. It alleviates a degree of stress and allows me to prioritize what I need to feel clear and shake out my emotions.

There are, of course, a great many activities and rituals that classify as self-care practices, and what works for one person may not work for another. I'm focusing here on what I know and sharing my experiences of my own self-care practices, but I'm not suggesting these are your only options. Take inspiration from my experiences, but lean into what you love. Making time for yourself to do anything you enjoy is an act of self-care, and if you can get some health benefits from it, even better.

Nature

I've always loved being outside, either surrounded by trees or looking out over the ocean, but it's not something I'd truly realized the power of until I began building it into my weekly routine. That time to myself before my day begins, time spent walking beneath the trees and spending quality time with my dog, immediately calms me. I feel surrounded by something much older than me that I want to experience fully, and it helps me breathe better and work through the things I need to think about. I'm present with myself in the moment in a way that comes to me much more naturally than it does in other situations. The trees, the grass, the water … They're constants. When I go home, they'll continue to be there, and I know I can count on them being there when I come back tomorrow. That thought in itself brings me great peace, especially in times of change.

Spending time in nature is recognized to come with significant health benefits, with physical effects including better breathing, an improved immune system, and improved sleep, but it has some profound benefits for our mental and emotional health, too. Sunlight helps relieve symptoms of depression, which is thought to be partly due to its power in helping the body produce Vitamin D and partly due to the fact that it triggers a release of serotonin from the brain, a hormone associated with boosting mood and making us feel calmer and more focused. The natural world offers a refuge when we need to recharge, soothing the senses with bird song, the smells of flowers and plants, and the beautiful natural landscapes—a welcome diversion from the overload of stimuli we're exposed to throughout the day; a diversion that manages to hold our attention without sucking out all our mental energy. Being outdoors also helps us soothe painful emotions and lean into pleasant ones like peace and happiness.

Physical Activity

For me, this is swimming and walking, but if you enjoy dancing, running, or cycling, that may be a better option for you. The physical benefits of exercise are well documented, and while they're important, they're not what I want to focus on here. Exercise comes with huge benefits for our mental and emotional health, too. It reduces stress and improves our sleep, and the release of endorphins it triggers makes us feel happier. Those endorphins also help to relieve anxiety; the effect is amplified by the fact that we're focused on the activity rather than whatever it is that's making us anxious. The increased blood flow delivers more oxygen and nutrients to different parts of the body, causing increased energy and improving cognitive function—both great assets in helping us tackle everything life has to throw at us.

I'll admit there was a time when I was so busy with everything else that exercise wasn't a priority for me, and since I've been building it into my routine, I've been noticing profound benefits. The biggest thing I have to get over every day is myself, and I feel that when I'm pushing myself in an activity. Perhaps I find it hard to get out the door, or maybe there's a hill coming up that I feel like I don't have the energy to tackle... but when I get past myself and push through those barriers, I remind myself that I can do this in every area of life. I remind myself of my own strength and determination, and that carries with me throughout the day. I feel stronger with every step. When I prioritize myself and make the time for physical activity, I feel like a warrior—and to me, that has nothing to do with going to war and everything to do with personal strength, determination, power, and resolve. I've pushed myself in a way that no one else will push me all day, and I've given myself a chance to feel my edges. I walk taller, and that drives me to keep going and push myself further. The boost in confidence and the mental resilience that it gives me isn't something I'd anticipated, and it's a huge motivator.

Massage

Our bodies hold onto stress, and massage therapy releases this stress, which has an effect on our anxiety levels. Research shows that it can reduce cortisol levels by as much as 30%, and this aids the body's ability to fight anxiety, as well as offering a safe space where we can escape our stressors and anxiety triggers for an hour. Studies also show a high correlation between massage and the reduction of symptoms of depression. Other benefits include improved concentration and focus, increased energy levels, and relief from insomnia, as well as the direct physical benefits of relieving tension in the muscles.

It's taken me years to be fully comfortable with massage, but I've always understood the physical health benefits because my body would be calmer and more relaxed after a session. The first few times I tried it, I found myself letting out emotion that had been pent up, and I certainly felt as much benefit to my mind as I did to my body. Now I have massages more routinely, I'm more in touch with my body and what it needs, and I have the confidence to ask for it—I'm more in concert with the masseuse, rather than letting them lead as I have done in the past. I have the power to choose my experience, and since I realized this, I've been able to reap the full range of benefits offered by massage.

Floating

Floating anywhere is relaxing, but what I'm referring to here is a flotation tank. I've only done this a couple of times, but the benefits I've felt have been profound. Flotation tanks or baths are filled with salt water. Lighting is minimal and atmospheric, and if there's sound, it's generally soothing music. The idea is that you're cut off from the lights and sounds of the outside world as the water holds you, allowing you to relax every part of your body. The water is heavy with Epsom salt, which provides buoyancy to enable easy floating. Health benefits include improved sleep quality, decreased pain, enhanced muscle relaxation, and a reduction in stress and anxiety. In the couple of sessions I've had, I've felt my body relax every muscle at once, allowing for complete relaxation and a release of pressure in my entire body. It brought me a sense of peace, and I was able to relax and tap into my gratitude. Some of that, I discovered, is also situational—sharing that experience with someone you can trust can amplify that benefit, allowing you to feel safe and at ease so that you can access everything it can offer you. I've learned a lot about what I need to feel safe over the last few years, and this has been a big one.

Sound Baths

A sound bath generally involves sitting in a relaxed position while traditional percussion and wind instruments are played to create overlapping vibrations designed to produce a soothing effect. The idea is that you reach a deep state of relaxation, shutting down your fight-or-flight reflex. Research into the health benefits of sound baths is still ongoing, but studies suggest they have the power to reduce tension, anxiety, and anger. There is also evidence to suggest a decrease in physical pain and improvements in heart rate and blood pressure. I'm still exploring what sound baths can do for me. My first experience was more difficult, and I found the sounds, particularly in conjunction with it being a communal experience, a little overwhelming, so it took me a while to get to a state of relaxation. My second experience was better, and

I was able to give in to the sounds and the calm lighting, allowing my mind to relax and letting me observe the thoughts and feelings that came up for me. It was a peaceful experience and not one that I found heavily emotional. I walked out of there feeling like I'd been meditating for an hour.

These last couple of activities—the sound bath and the flotation—are treatments I've been doing at my cousin Jenny's wellness center: Stella Luna Wellness Center, located in Cleveland. This is an example of a business that has thrived since it was first set up, and I'm so thankful for that. Creating the business has been an incredibly important part of Jenny's own healing journey, and the fact that she has curated a space that helps other people with theirs warms my heart.

Prioritizing self-care has given me the space and level of care for myself I needed in order to safely allow myself to feel everything that comes up for me without wallowing in negative emotions. It allows me to access the balance of being able to feel and cry my way through those emotions and move myself through them to get to a place of peace.

TALKING IT THROUGH

Getting comfortable with feeling your emotions is a huge part of the equation, but it's also important to be able to talk about them and to have someone you trust to do that with. I have people in my life who play that role, and I also speak to a counselor every few weeks.

Talk therapy is not only a valuable form of support; it offers us important information, too. My counselor regularly offers up nuggets of wisdom or ways of looking at the world that I take forward into every area of my life. A great example of this was when she showed me how to reframe a situation so that I could focus on my gratitude for all that was good rather than getting bogged down by the negatives. She shared a technique that involved rephrasing the thought, "I have to do x, y, and z," to "I *get* to do x, y, and z." That simple change in wording has huge power. Yes, it's true that I have to get my car fixed, but wow, aren't I lucky to have a car and the means to take care of it? I *get* to have my car fixed so that it can do all the things in my life that being able to drive helps me with. Her perspective through talk therapy, as an outsider, is one I can't get from any other area of life, and those reflections are incredibly valuable.

Talking to a therapist is healing and empowering. It reminds you that you can heal from trauma, and the very act of seeking it and making the effort to learn and get better in itself gives you a great sense of power. It teaches you how to acknowledge and manage your most difficult emotions, and that has a powerful effect on both you and the people around you. Talk therapy, if you give yourself to it fully, gives you a chance to become the best version of yourself, and I'm grateful to have it in my life.

EMOTIONAL ALCHEMY

The word "alchemy" refers to a process of transformation that seems magical. We see it in science, medicine, and cooking all the time. Let's take the example of an onion soaked in lemon juice. The acid in the lemon works to break down the compounds in the onion that cause the pungent flavor, releasing a sweet, delicate flavor and milder taste that you can't access until those cells have been broken down.

The combination of all the systems I've put in place to prioritize self-care and look after my mental and physical health has helped me to become an emotional alchemist. I'm able to acknowledge my pain and look at what I can learn from it, taking it forward into every element of my life. It's making a conscious effort not to shy away from what I've experienced and allowing myself to face the pain that has allowed me to turn it into peace. That doesn't mean it's easy, and it doesn't mean it doesn't hurt. It takes huge strength and courage to stand strong against those waves of painful emotions, and I find I'm fighting myself to get to peace almost every day, but the payoff is well worth it. Becoming an emotional alchemist is an ongoing process, just as prioritizing self-care is. You can't indulge in one single act of self-care, like going swimming or for a massage, and expect the benefits to last forever, nor can you sit with your pain just once and expect it all to go away afterward. You have to keep showing up and putting the work in. It doesn't make the pain less painful, but what you do is build up your strength to handle it, and your skills to use it as a force of positivity in your life. *That* is being an emotional alchemist; that is taking charge of your peace and healing.

➤ Tricks for Your Emotional Alchemy Bag

To help you get started with radical acceptance, try this exercise. The goal is to accept your lack of control over a particular situation and respond to it mindfully instead of giving in to your emotional reaction.

1. Determine the situation you're finding painful. Write notes about it. What happened before that situation, and how did the events unfold? What emotions did you feel?
2. Consider the role your own behavior played in the situation. Describe your actions, and think about how they influenced events. Next, consider how the actions and behaviors of others influenced those events. Try to identify what you had control over and what you didn't.
3. Consider how you reacted to the situation and the effect of your reactions on your emotions.
4. Think about how your reactions influenced other people. How did they behave in response?
5. Think about how you could behave more mindfully in the future if the same situation were

to arise. How could you respond instead of reacting emotionally?

Radical acceptance isn't an instant cure or a quick fix. It's an approach to managing difficult situations and using them to help you grow and reach a place of peace little by little. It's one step at a time, getting stronger with every forward movement.

4

STRONGER AND BETTER EVERY DAY: MASTERING YOUR POWER

"I want to thank me for just being me at all times. Snoop Dogg, you a bad motherfucker."

— SNOOP DOGG

There's a mantra I heard in a YouTube video once that I try to say to myself every morning: "Stronger every day in every way." Repeating it is a simple way for me to remind myself what I want and shape the experience I want to have. As I say it, I believe it, and it motivates me to take steps to achieve it. This is an example of positive self-talk.

HOW YOU TALK TO YOURSELF MATTERS

Our internal dialogue is powerful. When you talk to yourself negatively, you'll feel bad about yourself as you move through your life, but if you engage in positive self-talk, you'll open yourself up to improved self-esteem and confidence, and the transformative effects of this are incredible. When we're navigating difficulties, most of us have a tendency to focus on the negative elements of our experience, but this is the exact time it's most important to force yourself to think more optimistically. If you can do that, you'll find it much easier to deal with the challenges ahead of you. Intentionally shaping your thoughts to contain positive self-talk is a powerful way to identify and promote hope and joy.

It's very often the case that we've been cultivating a negative pattern of self-talk without even realizing it. We remember the negative things we've been told throughout our lives, particularly those that have lingered since childhood, playing on repeat in our minds and fueling a feeling of self-doubt, fear, and guilt. But studies have shown that positive self-talk is good for your performance, your relationships, and your mental health—and with a little work, it's something we can adopt.

This is something I've actively worked on, and I've seen its power. I had been engaging in negative self-talk for many years before I recognized that it was holding me back and preventing me from accessing all the peace and joy available to me. I would regularly tell myself that I was an asshole when I asked for what I needed, and I did this for years before I finally realized that all I was doing was perpetuating a myth about myself—a myth that I had talked myself into believing so much that I even warned people about it when I first met them. The result was that I was creating that expectation and inviting people to see me standing up for myself as me being an asshole. I've been working on reframing this. I'm not an asshole for asking for what I need, and I never have been.

Reprogramming yourself is like any other routine. Rather than it working immediately, you have to allow yourself to gradually reframe your negative thinking, and over time, you'll come to believe it. It's what you've chosen to embody. I still catch myself falling into old patterns of negative self-talk, and I learned a technique in counseling that helps me to deal with it. I visualize that negative self-talk spilling out of my ear to the person I'm talking to, and that helps me to hear it from the outside. I would never talk that way to someone else, and thinking of those phrases coming out of me, I realized that it wasn't serving me to beat myself up that way either, so it's easier to recognize it and shift. It still happens—after all, growth is an ongoing process—but I'm much more likely to recognize it and change my behavior now. I know there are times when negative self-talk has held me back because I've seen it shift since I started working on it. In situations where I had more work to do to reach the goal, I would tell myself that I wasn't there because I wasn't good enough, and it would discourage me from pushing myself further. When I reframed my thinking, I began to see not reaching the goal as a signpost showing me what I needed to do to improve. It changed my experience, and I was able to do the work I needed to in order to achieve that goal. I saw the benefits of making incremental changes, and in doing so, those goals that had seemed unattainable in the past gradually became things that I absolutely knew I could achieve.

The good news is, however, that this is a habit we can overcome with positive self-talk. It takes some work though—it requires us to notice instances of negative self-talk and turn them around before they stick. Experts recommend writing down examples of the way we talk to ourselves negatively as they arise in order to help us identify our patterns and think of more helpful things we could say instead. For example, "This is too difficult," could become "This sounds like a challenge," and "I always mess everything up," might become, "If it doesn't go right, I can learn from my mistakes." The benefits we stand to get if we can do this are quite remarkable. Simply by changing the way we speak to ourselves, we can eliminate self-doubt, improve our mood, and reduce our stress levels—and on those days when it's a struggle to keep going, it's a huge motivator. To really make the most of those positive effects, experts recommend using the second-person pronoun "you" when you're addressing yourself. This outside perspective helps you to regulate your emotions, thoughts, and behaviors in times of hardship.

The biggest hurdle I've found in working through this myself is recognizing instances of negative self-talk in the first place. Some of them are so ingrained that they've become a standard operating procedure, and those are the ones that are hardest to weed out. For example, I know someone who was navigating a complicated relationship situation, and she kept saying, "I don't want to lose them." I was able to see it in her much more clearly than she was at the time, and I encouraged her to reframe it and instead say, "I want to keep them." She said that as soon as she started changing the way she was thinking about it, she felt a much greater sense of control and clarity and was able to actively take steps to make sure her relationship with that person was nurtured. It gave her a clearer idea of what she *did* want—something that was much easier to control than the thing she didn't want.

EMBODYING CONFIDENCE

The same principle applies to how you hold yourself. Social psychologist Amy Cuddy recommends that everyone spends two minutes a day power posing—i.e., adopting poses associated with power, confidence, and success. These are strong poses with the head held high and the chest lifted. Cuddy has conducted studies that have shown an increase in testosterone and a decrease in cortisol levels when these stances are adopted, as well as a higher likelihood of taking risks. Individuals practicing her methods have reported greater confidence, improved performance, and greater success. I can attest to this myself—I've run through power poses before I've had to go into big meetings, and I've found that my confidence has improved and my warrior feeling has been ignited.

SHARING ENERGY WITH THE UNIVERSE

We can take this a step further and extrapolate it to look at the power of the energy we put into the universe. We can't control events that happen to us, but we can control our experience and make changes to invite more positive circumstances.

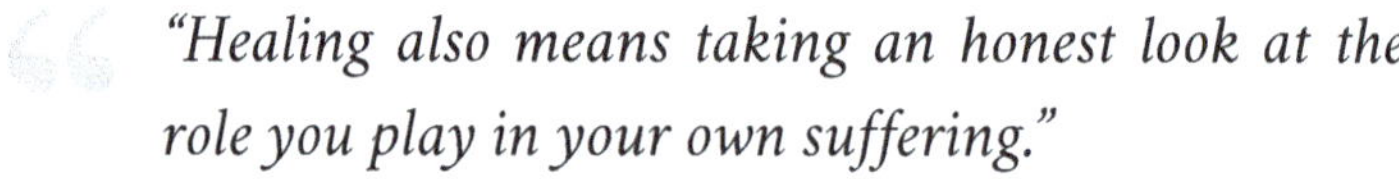

"Healing also means taking an honest look at the role you play in your own suffering."

— UNKNOWN

The Law of Attraction

The philosophy behind the law of attraction is that thoughts are a form of energy, and positive energy is a magnet for success in any area. Therefore, thinking positive thoughts and emitting positive energy is a way to manifest positive experiences. The central principle to this philosophy is that like attracts like—our thoughts attract results that reflect them, and if those thoughts are negative, it's negative experiences that will be attracted to us. Removing the negative elements of our lives allows us to make room for more positive things, but it's important, too, to recognize that there's always something you can do to improve your situation in the present moment. The law of attraction says that rather than focusing on our dissatisfaction within a given moment, our energy would be better spent on finding ways to get the best out of that moment as it is. In essence, we create our own reality by defining the positive we see. Whatever we focus on is what we'll attract into our life.

There may not be any scientific research to back up the law of attraction, but it's something I became interested in after watching the 2006 movie *The Secret*, and in trying to apply its principles, I've certainly found it to be true. It isn't always easy to shift your energy to a positive place, particularly during tumultuous times, but there are a few strategies you can employ to help you. It starts, as it so often does for me, with gratitude. Be grateful for what you have, and visualize what you want to see happening. Make yourself focus on the positives of any situation and recognize negative thoughts as they arise, reframing them as necessary to cultivate more positive energy. You can also use positive affirmations to help with this.

I've heard criticisms leveled at *The Secret* and about this way of thinking more times than I can tell you, and I get it, but I think that what it comes down to is that you have to take an active role in shaping your experience. I've heard people scoff at the idea that simply believing we'll get what we want will take us to our goals, but I think that's missing the point somewhat. It's not our attitude alone that shapes our experience but the proactive behaviors we apply as a result of that attitude. It's the action that creates change. Belief alone will get you nowhere, but it's a powerful driving force for the actions that will. We also have to recognize that there are some things that are beyond our control. Illnesses, layoffs, and personal tragedies aren't things we have any power over—but what we can control is our response to those circumstances.

Inviting Positive Energy Into Your Life

This is all good theory, but trust me, I know how difficult it is to embody that positive energy all the time. Life will test you, and as I've made the changes I've needed to make over recent years, I've had to battle hard to make sure I'm putting out the energy I want to see in the world. It can be done, however, and we've already touched on some of the things that will help you to do it. A key thing to remember is that staying optimistic doesn't mean ignoring negativity —in fact, as we've seen in our discussion of radical acceptance, we need to embrace that negativity in order to move forward. The secret lies in putting in measures to help you revive your positive energy when things get tough.

Spending time in nature is a great starting point for doing this, and as I mentioned in the last chapter, this is something that works really well for me. Being in the present, surrounded by all that natural beauty, reminds me of everything I have and gives me the perspective I need to know that everything will be okay and I'm right where I need to be, no matter how hard things might be that day. Really, any act of self-care is a good way to go—something that allows you to celebrate who you are and remind you of what's truly important. I find it much easier to lock into a positive mindset on the days that I've given myself that time.

Performing acts of kindness is another good way to cultivate positive energy. I remember being in the grocery store once when a lady knocked some vegetables down from a display, trying to reach what she wanted. I told her it happens to me all the time and joked that it's like they deliberately set them up that way for it to happen. I helped her pick up the fallen produce, and the smile on her face and her gratitude for support from a stranger in a moment when she felt embarrassed was everything I needed in that moment. It was such a small moment, but it made a huge difference to both of us in the few minutes it lasted. Gratitude is another big one—taking a moment to appreciate all those small things is powerful, and it can affect our mood and the energy we give off immediately.

Taking breaks is helpful too—and I don't just mean a break from work or cleaning your house—I mean a break from whatever it is that's troubling you. Sometimes, for me, that looks like a nap, but it could equally be a walk outside or an hour watching your favorite TV show—just something to give yourself a break from your thoughts and feelings for long enough to shift your energy. Surrounding yourself with positive people helps too, so that break could involve a coffee with a friend who you know always lifts your spirits. Research indicates that stress is contagious, so if you surround yourself with other people's stressed-out energy, the chances are, it's going to affect you too… but if you surround yourself with positive people, that's going to rub off on you. It may also give you a chance to talk through your problems, and that can be very helpful for getting perspective and moving yourself back toward a more positive place.

Looking for the bright side is a good move, too. Don't get me wrong, I know that isn't always easy, but usually, there's at least one thing, however small, that you can view in a positive light if you're determined to find it. Breathing exercises help me here. Sometimes, I need to calm myself down before I can get to a place where I can find the positive. Take a few deep breaths until you feel your body slow down and find your center again. Use this moment to recognize your negativity and try to shift yourself away from it. That positive self-talk we've been discussing is a good tool to bring out in this moment, as is journaling, which has always been a good outlet for me when I've needed to get things straight in my mind.

Lastly, never underestimate the power of a good night's rest. Research has shown that even a small amount of sleep deprivation can have a significant impact on your state of mind, and I can certainly tell you that I've found it much harder to maintain a positive mindset when I haven't had enough sleep. When you rise in the morning, make a conscious effort to move through your day mindfully. When you're fully present in the moment as it is, you'll find the joy that comes to you much more easily than when you focus on future events you may be worried about or dwell on things that happened in the past.

THE POWER OF MUSIC

If you've ever found yourself crying over a saucepan when a sad song comes on the kitchen radio or dancing around the living room to that one song that always gets you really pumped up, it'll be no surprise to hear that music affects us emotionally. In fact, composers who work on movies use this all the time to elicit the emotional response they want us to have. There's science behind this: upbeat, happy music triggers a chemical release of serotonin and dopamine in our brains, and calming music causes the body and mind to relax. It works the other way around too—our mood has just as much chance of influencing the music we choose to play as the music has of affecting our mood.

Dopamine is a natural antidepressant, which is why music is sometimes used as a tool in therapy to address cognitive, psychological, and communicative issues. Music also affects your heart rate, either slowing it down with relaxing beats or speeding it up with a high-beat tempo. So, if you're stressed out and your heart rate is up, you can slow yourself down by listening to calming music. Both blood pressure and stress levels have been shown to be reduced due to the effect of music, and its ability to distract us from a stressful situation is incredible.

We can also use music to push us in the direction we want to go. If we're struggling with feelings of sadness, we can choose music that will make us feel energized and happy. I turn to music to help shake myself out of a mood I don't want to be in or to calm myself down when I'm feeling anxious. Almost every part of the brain is used when we listen to music, and neuroscientists have found that a series of chemical processes are activated, including an increase in oxytocin and serotonin and an activation of the brain's reward centers. Music communicates with us on levels that only it can, and the chemical reactions in the brain that it inspires show that it literally has the power to change our mood. Equally, though, we can use music to match our emotional state. Although there are times when we want to move away from that state, there are others when it's therapeutic to lean into our emotions, and music can help us to do that in a way that connects us with the artist and helps us feel less alone.

Memory has a huge role to play in our relationship with music, too, and we often remember songs more easily than we remember facts or words. The pattern of the melody is retained in the hippocampus, which is also the part of the brain that stores our memories. When we listen to a particular song, our past memories of it are triggered, and we remember so much more than the song —we also remember feelings we've had and the contexts in which we've heard it. That song delivers a complete parcel of sound, memory, and emotion. With any song we know well, we feel the stories associated with it and, therefore, a sense of familiarity with ourselves. We see our inner self reflected back, and although sometimes a song may trigger a memory we find painful to think about, it connects us with an emotion that is part of our story, part of who we are. Music is a mirror, allowing us to connect each part of ourselves with others and see our whole selves reflected back. It is a tool we can use to make order out of chaos. Our brains recognize the patterns and rhythms in the music, and this is soothing. It can make the chaos in our lives feel more organized and easier to control.

My musical tastes span multiple genres, and I find music that speaks to me everywhere. In fact, sometimes it's more like it finds me exactly when I need it. I've always been a huge fan of the Foo Fighters. Maybe it's Dave Grohl's resilience all those years ago that showed me the way, or maybe it's the music; either way, I know I'm stronger for it. The music gets into my soul and moves me from within. It connects me to myself and to everyone I've shared it with, and I can use it to reset myself when I need it. I love music that makes me want to join in, that makes me want to be loud and not shut up when something needs to be said. Music that can inspire that feeling is incredible.

Creating positive energy, however you approach it, gives you the power to take yourself out of your current emotional state and direct your energy into a more positive feeling. Again, it's emotional alchemy. It gives you the feeling that you can control and help the world… and when you have that feeling, you realize you can, starting one step at a time with your own experience and what you choose to do with your time and skills.

➤ Tricks for Your Emotional Alchemy Bag

Create a positive mantra for yourself that you can use to set yourself up for the day and invite positive energy in. Here are some ideas to get you started:

➤ *I'm proud of who I am, and I'm enough just the way I am.*
➤ *Life is unfolding like a beautiful story.*
➤ *I can achieve anything I want to when I give it the time and effort.*

> *I am exactly where I'm meant to be, and every step takes me further.*
> *Everything that's happened in the past has led me to this present moment.*

As you build your resilience, getting stronger and better every day, you equip yourself to deal with the challenges that come up—and there *will* be challenges. Healing is a continuous process, and there will always be triggers that bring up those difficult emotions. We'll look at some of those things in a moment.

STRONGER EVERY DAY IN EVERY WAY

"We make a living by what we get, but we make a life by what we give."

— WINSTON CHURCHILL

Just as healing is a continuous process, so is learning, and for me, learning is a vital part of growth. I always want to arm myself with new skills, feed my brain with new information, and find out what I can do better. And this impacts my healing, too. The more I learn about the world and other people, the more I can build up my toolkit and develop new practices that help me on my journey.

And this is where I'd like to ask for your input. Part of what I want from my life is to know that I've been of service and that my experiences have helped others, and I want to know how I can do that better. I want to know where I'm getting it right, and I want to know what I can do to deliver even more value.

So, I'd like to take this opportunity to ask for your feedback, and you can give that in the form of a review.

By leaving your honest feedback on Amazon, you'll let me know how this book has helped you and what I can do to make the next one even better.

My books are journeys to write for me, and I want the lessons I've clawed for to be valuable resources to support you on your journey. Let me know what you've gained from reading them, and if you have thoughts about what I can do to improve them, don't be afraid to tell me.

Stronger every day in every way: that's my goal … and your feedback is so valuable to me in building that strength and using it to serve others.

5

THE THINGS THAT SHAKE US: DEALING WITH REMINDERS AND MEMORIES

"It seems that everywhere I turn there is a reminder to be found, and I have come to a place where they no longer break my heart; they make me smile."

— DAVE GROHL

When we lose someone, there are objects that we carry forward that remind us of them—whether that's something that was left to us, something we shared with them, or something they once gave us. That's particularly the case if you share your life with someone and you carry forward objects that were once shared. I've struggled with this a lot over the years, and there are certain things I've let go of along the way—objects, for example, that belonged to my mom and brought up painful feelings when I looked at them, which I assessed would bring more joy to someone else and donated. This was a powerful act of letting go, knowing my mom would be happy for them to go somewhere that they would be used and enjoyed. This isn't always the case. There are some things you will always want to hold on to because they were important to someone you loved, and you know it was important to them for you to keep them. And there are some things it just isn't practical to get rid of— I'm not going to throw my iPhone out, for example, just because the person who showed me how to use it isn't in my life anymore. Am I not going to use a device that's become important to my daily functioning just because I've lost my relationship with that person? The idea seems ridiculous, and the chances are, if we did that with everything, we'd have very little left we could use.

LINKING OBJECTS

Sentimental objects that are passed down from loved ones are sometimes known as "linking objects"—they're objects that connect us to the person we've lost, and they can be very important in healing, allowing us to feel closer to them. Usually, these objects were owned by that person, but this isn't always the case. Sometimes, they're simply objects that evoke memories of them. These objects can lose their significance over time, which can sometimes lead to feelings of guilt, but this is a healthy part of accepting your new reality. Not all objects lose their significance, though; some are passed down through the generations. This is largely dependent on what the item is and how significant it was to your relationship with the person you lost. I kept my mom's things in storage for years before I was ready to go through them. I went through them three or four times over the years. I only have a handful of things that were hers left because, for me now, 20 years later, it isn't about the stuff; it's about the memories she's left with me, and that's what I needed to deal with. Her stuff was just an extension of that; it wasn't her. Her memory and strength live on in me, not in her things. Keeping a lot of her possessions around me would have done me more harm than good, and this is something to be aware of with linking objects. They can give rise to painful emotions, and when it no longer feels like they connect you to the person you've lost, this can include anxiety, guilt, and shame. Many people find themselves at a crossroads here: part of them wants to move on, but another part feels the need to preserve the memory of the person they've lost.

A helpful question to ask yourself in this situation is: "What purpose is this object serving?" Perhaps you thought it was connecting you to your loved one, but maybe the reality is that it's doing more to keep you buried in your grief. If what's really happening is that you're using that linking object to deny the reality of your loss, you're stifling your healing process. On the other hand, asking yourself this question could reveal that keeping the object is allowing you to honor your loved one. One thing I still have of my mom's is a ring, which I wear on my index finger. It makes me feel like she's close to me, a part of every moment in my life she never got to see. It's something she wore for a time, and it's part of my memory of her. Wearing it is a way I can honor her and, at the same time, make it a part of my own identity. I think she'd be happy with that.

If you realize that your linking object is serving to feed your pain more than it is to honor your loved one, it's probably time to let that object go. This is a tough decision to make, but it can also be a very important step in the healing process. I know it was for me.

When it comes to items carried forward from a relationship that's no longer in your life, similar principles apply. For sentimental items, it's easier in some ways—practical objects like my iPhone may trigger memories, but they're not sentimental in and of themselves. These items we just have to learn to live with, and the good news is that we can—objects like phones play so many other roles in our lives that, over time, those associations will fade to the point that they're no longer painful to recall.

LETTING GO OF OBJECTS

When I was sorting through my mom's things, I found it helpful to remind myself that she was not her stuff. If, as I was, you're faced with a lot of things to sift through, you may find yourself wondering why you've held on to so much. That's okay, too—you had to wait until you were ready, and now you are. For each item, ask yourself why you're holding on to it. If it's linked to special memories, ask yourself if you could recall those memories without the object. Ask yourself whether it's useful, and if it is, would someone else get more from it than you do? If it isn't but you're not ready to let it go, could you repurpose it as something useful or do something creative to breathe new life into it? Make yourself three piles: one of the objects to donate, one of the objects you intend to keep, and one of the things you may need a little more time to think about.

For the things you decide are no longer serving you, a great option is to give them to other people in your life. I've done this with a few things, and it's comforting to know that they're still with people I love. It's also good if you have a friend who's in need of the thing you're trying to let go of—if you have your dad's side table, for example, and there's no place for it in your home, but your friend has told you they're looking for one, giving it to them is a win-win situation, and it makes letting go easier when you know that it's helping someone else out. If no one you know needs anything, you can do this by donating it to a goodwill store.

With your pile of undecided objects, or the ones you want to keep but don't really know what to do with, make a list of what you have and what you want to prioritize. Perhaps some have a place in your home, and others will need to be hidden away or put into storage. If you're thinking of putting things into storage, however, you may want to revisit the question of what purpose that object is fulfilling. I know some people who've found their way around this by taking photos of those objects so that they can revisit their memories without them taking up excess space in their homes.

Sometimes, the objects we're holding on to aren't things that are of any use to anyone else, and keeping them is only going to cause us pain. Items kept from past romances are good examples of this—it might be a tiny thing like the menu of the restaurant you went to on your first date; perhaps it's a love letter or a photograph that is too painful to keep. If you decide that items like this are causing you too much pain, making a ritual out of letting go of them can be very healing. Burning them in a safely controlled outdoor fire and consciously releasing the energy they were taking up inside you could allow you to purge the objects ceremoniously in a way that gives you some sense of closure.

INVOLUNTARY MEMORIES

Linking objects aren't the only things we bring forward that can be difficult to let go of. There are also those practical objects that remind us of someone—particular brands of a product, for example. There's a brand of menthol oil I like that triggers painful memories of what's been lost with the person who introduced me to it. But it's more complicated than that—it also reminds me of another brand rubbed on my chest when I had bronchitis in childhood. It's something that reminds me of my mom and being cared for. I've always used menthol oil, and since I was introduced to this particular brand, it's become the one I like. It was a ritual I had with someone else that's now become a ritual of my own. It's all a part of who I am, and I have to embrace that, allow myself to feel all the emotions that arise, and find a way forward. It's a sensory reminder—the memories are triggered not just by the physical bottle but by the smell and the sensation of the oil on my body. I feel the sadness associated with what's been lost every time I use the oil, yet I benefit from it, and it's a part of my own ritual now. To give that up would be giving up some of who I am—who I have become. It requires emotional alchemy, and it's still something I'm working on, practicing gratitude for the benefits it brings me and for the happy times that only now make me sad because they're in the past.

One of the reasons the menthol oil is particularly triggering for me is that it speaks to several senses. Smells can be especially painful when we're trying to move forward. Simply walking past someone in the street who's wearing the perfume someone we once loved used to wear can stir up long-forgotten memories and emotions. The power of involuntary memory has been well documented, with perhaps the most famous example being the Proustian

Rush. The phrase "involuntary memory" was coined by Marcel Proust in the novel *In Search of Lost Time*. He viewed it to contain the "essence of the past" and described his protagonist recalling a long-forgotten memory of being at his aunt's house as a child in the moment that he ate a madeleine soaked in tea. This memory then sparked a rush of other memories about the house itself and the town he spent time in as a child. Smell has the power to unlock memory and emotion, and research suggests that odors connect to emotion more closely than other sensory experiences. Indeed, clinicians have noted that smells relating to trauma (for example, blood or gas) can induce fear and anxiety-related memories in PTSD patients. The olfactory nerves are connected to the part of our brain that deals with memory and allows us to access memories from decades ago. Auditory, visual, and touch information doesn't pass through the same area of the brain, so while we may be reminded of something because of a sound or a picture, it's unlikely to be as visceral.

Involuntary memory can also be triggered by food—partly because smell is so heavily intertwined with taste. This is common after a relationship ends, particularly if you have memories of cooking with an ex-partner, where all the senses are involved. Specific dishes might remind you of that person and your relationship, and that can make eating them painful. The best thing to do in this situation is to try to reclaim the dish by changing an ingredient or a spice in order to alter the scent and flavor and make it new. If this isn't enough, it may be best to avoid that dish for a while and focus on enjoying the foods you'd stopped eating because your partner didn't like them.

The silver lining to this is that we can turn that involuntary memory into a conscious act of honoring our loved ones. I wrote about making French bread pizzas to honor my dad in *An Original Grief Guide.* The level of painful memory that triggers depends on my situation at the time and whether or not I planned it. Sometimes, it can make me miss him more, but the act itself is healing. My experience isn't always the same, but knowing that French bread pizzas make me think of him gives me a certain degree of control and a tool with which I can honor him.

Music can be another trigger for involuntary memory. Think of all the songs that remind you of a past relationship or of a particular person you've lost. Those songs can be very painful to listen to, and hearing them can trigger all kinds of memories and bring up strong emotions. This is something that's very present for me at the moment, and I'm consciously making an effort to ride that emotional wave and keep listening to the music. The more I can do that, the less involuntary those memories will be, and the more I'll be able to enjoy the music for what it is without being blindsided by the flurry of emotions associated with my memory of it.

Like smell, music helps shape our autobiographical memory. As we saw in the last chapter, music stimulates many parts of the brain, and it strengthens the detail contained in our memories—everything we felt, smelled, and tasted in a particular moment can be recalled by listening to a song. This is linked to survival programming, something that evolved to prevent us from making the same mistake twice—and this means there's no way to unlink a song from the memories we associate with it. But what we can do is create new memories and associations, and we can make a deliberate choice to listen to those painful songs and feel the emotions that come up for us. Again, this is radical acceptance.

There's a particular song that I shared with someone I love in a jovial way, and hearing that song now that they're no longer in my life, remembering those good memories, can be very painful. I heard it recently and took it in. I owned it, and I moved on. What's the alternative? Let it ruin my day? No, I'm going to choose to give the song its three minutes, feel it, and move on. I'm on the other side now, and I can still appreciate that song and the happy memories attached to it, even if there's a sadness in hearing it again now life has changed.

Songs can collect meanings over time, making the initial association less painful, but that can only happen if we allow them in. A lot of people experience this with Christmas songs. We hear the same Christmas songs every year, and we often associate them with someone we love who's no longer alive. That can be very hard when they sneak up on us during the holiday season, but over the years, repeated exposure means that while they may still force painful emotions to the surface, they'll also collect new memories of Christmas parties, events, and associations with new generations and their joy in Christmas.

DEALING WITH EMOTIONAL MEMORIES

Although some of those emotional experiences triggered by objects, music, and sensory input are painful, I want to be reminded of all the parts of me. If I'm to grow and move into a place of peace, I need to acknowledge and accept every part of my journey, everything that made me into who I am today and who I will be going forward. I need to let my guard down in order to let peace in. I want to be reminded of the changes that happen when a relationship ends so that I can honor that relationship, recognize and appreciate all that was good about it, and use what I've learned from it to move forward. I want to be the emotional alchemist because I plan to experience all the joy and peace that's available to me, and not allowing myself this growth robs me of that opportunity.

There's also a point to be made here about the value of passing stories and memories forward—think about the death of a family member and wanting to keep their stories alive for future generations. I know someone who has a ship's clock in their family. Only one person in the family left behind ever knew its original owner, but that clock comes with his history and stories, and if the clock hadn't been kept, those stories wouldn't have been passed down. What makes that clock even more special now is that everyone in the family hates it. It ticks loudly, and it's designed to measure nautical miles, so the ticking is fast, and it drives everyone crazy. It's become a family joke, and the banter around it has given it new stories, which will carry with it as it's passed forward to the next generation.

The immediate descendants may feel the pain associated with these objects, but as they're passed down, they're an important way of keeping family history alive. We have to keep feeling the thing.

> *"A memory without the emotional charge is called wisdom."*
>
> —JOE DISPENZA

When we have a strong emotional response to something, the brain forms a more detailed memory of it, and it sticks. This is where that survival programming comes in —by remembering the things that caused these strong, often painful, emotions, we're triggered to avoid similar situations and prevent the same thing from reoccurring. This effect is even stronger if the emotional memory has a story attached to it. The story provides the brain with a structure that's easier to remember… and as if that wasn't hard enough, we do it to ourselves. When we experience something that hurts us, we tend to go over and over it in our minds, feeding it with even more emotion and cementing it further. We end up creating even bigger narratives, which hurt us more. The extra complication here is that memory is fallible. It's impossible to remember everything accurately, so we just remember the key part of the experience, the part most closely related to our strongest emotions—and even those memories will deteriorate as time moves on. We fill in the gaps with our existing knowledge, and sometimes that means we make the memory feel even worse than it did when it happened.

There's a useful piece to this, though. Because our memories are flexible, we have the power to change the way we see them—and, consequently, we can change the way we feel about them, too. This means we can take the power away from those most difficult memories. Let's take the example of a breakup to see how we can do that.

Neutralizing a Memory

This process starts by reducing the power of the emotion related to the memory—for example, the intense pain you felt when your partner told you they wanted to end your relationship. Don't be afraid of that emotion; simply hold it, sit with it, and feel it. It was a natural human response at the time, but it doesn't have to carry the same weight moving forward. You're no longer in that moment, and you don't have to relive it. The goal is to see it for what it was, and that requires you to make a conscious decision to feel the emotion without holding on to it (hello again, radical acceptance).

The next step is to rewrite the story. If we hear something often enough, we tend to believe it—think back to that negative self-talk—I told myself I was an asshole for so long that I came to believe it was part of who I was… but just as I have been reframing that perception of myself and recognizing that it was never true, we have the power to rewrite the narrative. We know that the central events of our memories are true, but since the rest of it is mostly just our interpretation, we can challenge it, tinkering with it to change the memory of the breakup. If, for example, in the months leading up to that breakup, your ex had been pulling away and seemed less interested in you, you may have convinced yourself that there was someone else in the picture. You don't know this—this could be a detail you've added, and if you're not careful, it could become part of the narrative. You have power over that narrative. You don't have to focus on the part that is entirely based on your interpretation. You can instead tell yourself that you were growing apart during this time. It still hurts, but probably not as much as your partner cheating on you.

Doing this isn't taking away the significance of that memory, but it's taking away its power and giving it back to you. You still get to keep the lessons there are to take forward, and you still get to keep that piece of who you are… but you're able to take away some of what hurts you. You're choosing to see that memory in a more empowering way.

Stepping Away From the Past

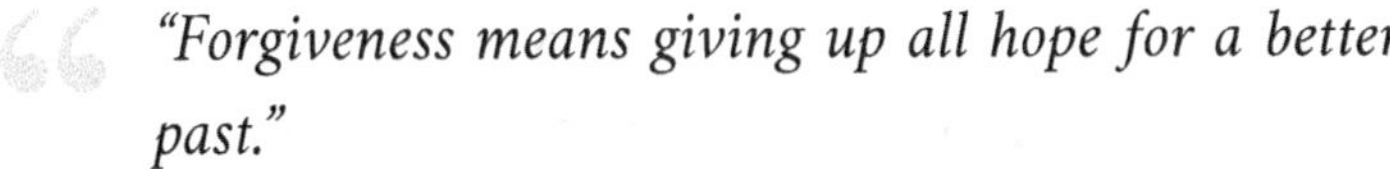 *"Forgiveness means giving up all hope for a better past."*

— LILY TOMLIN

In taking away the power of a memory, you're allowing it to become something you can put on the shelf. It's a story you can pick up and read whenever you want to, but you can choose when you do that. It doesn't have to be with you all the time. This is an image I picked up in therapy, and I've found it to be helpful in keeping those painful waves of emotion triggered by memories at bay. Leaving the past in the past is difficult, and it's something that takes a considerable amount of work. A lot of what we've covered already will help you to do this, but I've included some extra nuggets here for you, too:

- Stay away from places and people that trigger painful emotions.
- Make self-care a part of your daily routine.

- Spend your time with people who love and support you.
- Replace negative self-talk with positive self-talk.
- Allow yourself to feel your emotions.
- Stay away from social media for a while.
- Accept that you may never get the apology you're hoping to hear.
- Forgive yourself for your mistakes, and think about what you can learn from them.
- Let go of any resentment you have. Carrying it with you is only hurting you; it has no impact on the person you resent. Forgiveness is as much about your wellbeing as the other person's—if not more.
- Put your goals in writing: Make a plan for your forward moves.
- Refocus by practicing mindfulness.
- Practice gratitude, both for how far you've come and for everyone who's helped you get there.
- Make it your mission to make new memories.
- Acknowledge the past, but accept that it can't be changed. What matters now is how you move forward.

➤ Tricks for Your Emotional Alchemy Bag

To help you to focus on the present moment and accept reality as it is, try this exercise:

Make a list of the realities that you find distressing. Next to each one, write down the ways you can accept that reality objectively.

E.g., Distressing reality: *I feel isolated.*

Ways to accept that reality: *I feel isolated because I've moved to a new place and I haven't met anyone yet. To solve this, I can sign up for an activity I'm interested in, where I will meet people who have some of the same interests that I do. Over time, I will feel less isolated.*

———

Some of the most painful memories we have to work on leaving behind have to do with rituals we once shared with another person. Ritual is powerful, and that's why it plays such an important role after a death. It's a powerful tool for healing, and you can use it to arm you against those surprising emotions that knock the wind out of your sails when you're least expecting it.

6

RIDING THE WAVE: ARMING YOURSELF TO DEAL WITH SURPRISE EMOTIONS

"The best way out is always through."

— ROBERT FROST

If we refer to the Kübler-Ross model of grieving, we take acceptance to be the final stage of the process, and one of the dangers of relying on the model too much is that there can be the tendency to think we should be "better" by then.

Acceptance is not about being okay with what happened; it's about accepting the reality that it did. It's about living with what is rather than what you wish could be. Once you've suffered a loss, grief will always be a part of your life, and no matter how many years pass, you'll still be blindsided by grief on a random Tuesday. A smell, a song, or a flavor can come at you out of the blue, and suddenly, you'll be flooded with that same raw feeling you were dealing with right back at the beginning of the healing process. This is why repressing our emotions doesn't work—we can't deny our loss or stop those feelings from coming up. What matters is how we deal with them and how quickly we can get back to joy on the other side.

WHY DOES GRIEF COME IN WAVES?

Grieving is a big task for our brains. We can only process so much at once, and sometimes the weight of it triggers depression. This is what's known as complicated grief, but even when this doesn't happen, our brains can't do it all at once, and it will take time to work through different facets of the pain and accept the new reality. In the case of the death of a loved one, it can take time for that new reality to take hold; you may find yourself calling for them, momentarily forgetting they're no longer there. Adjusting to a reality without someone you love in it is hard, no matter the nature of your loss. Everything you used to do together is going to be hard and unfamiliar when you face it alone, and significant dates like holidays and birthdays will remind you of their absence. This often triggers anxiety, which may be characterized by worrying, a racing mind or heart, muscle tension, and fatigue. Healing isn't a linear process—you go back and forth, and there are triggers everywhere you turn. Maybe it's seeing something of theirs around the house or walking past a place filled with your memories together; maybe it's those smells we talked about or a surprise attack from a song on the radio. All of these things bring fresh waves of grief, and while they do become less frequent and easier to bounce back from over time, they never truly go away.

Grief Triggers

Grief triggers are deeply personal, and while there are several common ones that most of us experience, they could be anything, and you could find yourself faced with some surprising ones. This came up for me recently. I was doing the laundry in a new machine that requires you to add the detergent from the top once the water has started filling up. Ever since I've been using that machine, I've swished the water around in a particular way, and there was one moment when it just hit me: I do it that way because my mom did. I also heard my mom's words as I wiped around the inside of the drum after doing a load: "You can't get clean clothes out of a dirty washer." Both of these moments had me in tears as though my grief was fresh, yet I do laundry all the time, and this has never happened to me before. Moments like these are painful, and you can't plan for them, but I'm thankful for them too. They remind me that she's always with me, and sometimes, when memories like that come up, they don't make me cry; they make me smile. Just as we can't have summer without living through winter, we can't feel the good things without living through the bad ones.

You can't prepare for triggers like this, but there are some common ones that most people find difficult, and while you can't stop them from affecting you, you can arm yourself with the knowledge that they happen, and there's something helpful in that predictability. Some of them are things we've already discussed, and the chances are, you've run into them all already:

- **Music:** This could be a song you shared with someone you love, a song they liked, or a song with lyrics that encapsulate your loss or your feelings about them.
- **Smells:** Perfumes, foods, detergents, flowers … Trigger smells can come from anywhere, and they hit you at surprising moments. I know someone who was taken aback in a bar once because the smell of the roasted meat on the menu combined with the smell of bleach from an area that had been cleaned reminded her of her grandmother's house. The bleach alone wouldn't have done it, and nor would the meat, but the combination blindsided her.
- **Places:** Particularly when you live in the same area you shared with the person you lost, triggering places can be all around. There are the places you visited together, the ones where you shared special memories, and there are the mundane ones—the grocery store where you shopped together or the street you walked up

every day to get to work. Then there are the places they never got to see but you know they would have loved. It can be terribly sad knowing how much they would have enjoyed being there. My mom asked me to take her ashes with me wherever I went, and this has helped me to deal with that. On a recent trip to Greece, there was solace in scattering some of her and my dad's ashes into the sea and knowing they were there with me. It was a beautiful moment. The sunlight hit a distant island at the exact moment that they started floating out toward it, and the feeling I was left with was a mixture of joy and gratitude. The sadness was there, but because I allowed myself to feel it, I was also able to let the light in, feel their presence, and enjoy the moment.

- **Photos:** There are the physical photos you have from the days before digital images, and there are the ones you have on your laptop or your phone. Pictures of a shared life can be very challenging, especially at the beginning of the grieving process. Surprising reminders from Facebook or your phone can catch you unawares, too. For me, moving photos off my phone and taking a break from social media have been extremely helpful in having control over when I want to look at those memories. I want to see them… I just want to be able to choose *when* I see them. Right before work on a Thursday is not that time.

- **Possessions:** The things you shared or the things your loved one has left behind are particularly difficult in the beginning, but they can trigger you even years down the line. This is one of the reasons I let go of a lot of my mom's stuff.

- **Anniversaries and holidays:** These are universal triggers for anyone who has lost someone. The empty chair at the table on Thanksgiving or the birthday card you no longer get to send will rise every year, but as time goes on, you'll be able to enjoy some of the happy memories that surface, and though there will be sadness, there will be joy too.

- **New people and things:** For every new joy you experience as you go forward, there may be a sadness that your loved one never got to share it. Perhaps it's a new partner you wish your mom had been able to meet or a loft renovation you wish your dad could have seen; perhaps it's a new baby in the family whom you wish your parents could have been grandparents to. These things will always arise, and as life moves on, there will always be reminders of what your loved one missed.

- **Things people say:** We're particularly sensitive when we're grieving, and sometimes someone will say something that will trigger a swelling in our pain. Often, this is very well-meaning, sometimes even innocuous, but it still affects us and reminds us of what we've lost.

Surprise Attacks of Grief

You can't plan for those surprise attacks of grief, but you can arm yourself with the knowledge of what they might look like. Of course, no two people experience grief in exactly the same way, but these are common experiences to be aware of:

- **Tearfulness:** There's a deep sadness that claws right into your gut when you lose someone you love. When you think of a future without them in it, the tears come, and sometimes it feels like they won't ever stop. Try to keep in mind that allowing those tears to flow will help you to heal, and let yourself walk through the moment and feel what you need to.
- **Apathy:** Sometimes, it can feel like you're just going through the motions with barely enough energy to make it through the day. It's hard to care about anything when you're putting everything you've got into surviving. This will pass, and you'll find your interests and energy coming back to you with time. Grieving takes a lot of energy; it makes sense that there's not a lot left to give to anything else.

- **Grumpiness:** Patience isn't always our greatest strength when we're processing a loss. You may find yourself irritable as you try to adjust to your new reality, both with others and with yourself. Self-care is a useful tool here—finding a way to physically release some of that frustration will help you manage it.
- **Mental fog:** Your attention and concentration may take a knock, which can be very distressing, particularly if you're also tackling the responsibilities associated with a death. Try not to worry if you find yourself unable to do the things you're usually capable of. You're not going crazy; you're grieving. Let go of tasks that aren't essential, and don't place so much expectation on yourself.
- **Disrupted sleep:** Grief can take a physical toll as well as a mental one, and this is often seen in your ability to get quality sleep. Dreams can be vivid, and they often involve the person you've lost, leaving you to wake and face the reality of their absence afresh. This is your mind doing its thing and processing your loss. It hurts like hell, but it's helping you to heal.
- **Involuntary memories:** You may find yourself recalling memories you didn't even know you remembered—things that happened decades ago and that you haven't thought of in years. These can trigger more memories, a pathway of linked

stories that lead you back into the past. I think the most helpful thing to do when this happens is to focus on the memory rather than the sadness around it. It's a way you can travel back in time and appreciate those moments for what they were.

- **Panic attacks:** These seem like they come from nowhere, and suddenly, your body's pumping with adrenaline, you're short of breath, and your heart's racing. They can last anywhere from five minutes to half an hour, but they *will* pass—and we'll look at how to cope with them in a moment.

Decompressing After Experiencing a Grief Trigger

There may be a temptation to throw yourself into something else to try to distract yourself from a trigger, or you may find yourself at the opposite end of the spectrum and find it difficult to do anything when that wave of sadness hits you. Try these steps to help you walk through the moment and back to a sense of peace:

- **Acknowledge your feelings:** You might feel embarrassed, or you might think that if you ignore it, it will go away, but it's important to acknowledge how you feel. Without doing so, you'll be unable to access the tools you need to help you through the moment.

- **Allow yourself time to settle:** Once you've acknowledged the trigger, give yourself time to reset. Perhaps you need to splash your face with cold water; maybe you need to pull the car over. Whatever it is, you need to focus on what you need in that moment rather than trying to push through.
- **Take deep, slow breaths:** Grief sets off a chain of reactions in the body, and you may find your heart rate elevated and your breath short. Slow, diaphragmatic breathing will help to reduce your heart rate and get your breathing back to normal.
- **Seek support if you need it:** If you're further through the process and you've experienced the trigger a few times, perhaps you can handle this alone, but doing this in the beginning can leave you feeling very isolated. This was a feeling I experienced recently on Father's Day, which crept up on me by surprise and sent me down a spiral of sadness. Even though a big part of me wanted to hide, I called someone I love and talked to her about what I was going through. It didn't cure the feeling, but it did help me to move through it and get to the next step I needed to take to feel better.
- **Rest:** Those bouts of fatigue can still happen years down the line, and they may surface when you run into a trigger. Your body and your mind need rest, and it's okay to take it—even if it's Sunday afternoon and you still have all the ironing left to

do. You are more important than creaseless clothes.

- **Note the trigger:** Particularly if it's the first time you've experienced it, it's important to take note of what triggered your grief. This will help you to prepare for it and know how to cope in the future. My mom's comment about not being able to get clean clothes out of a dirty washer has come up a few times since it hit me that day, and now that I'm prepared for it, I'm able to smile at the memory—in fact, it almost feels like I get to say it before she does, and there's some joy in the idea of sharing that with her.

Coping With a Panic Attack

Panic attacks can be scary, especially if you're not used to having them. You can't protect against them entirely, but if you find that you're having them frequently, it may help to avoid caffeine, alcohol, and nicotine for a while. Exercise, which is known to reduce stress, can also help, as can eating regularly to make sure your blood sugar levels stay stable.

If you do find yourself experiencing a panic attack, try the following techniques to move through it:

- **Take slow, deep breaths:** Breath in through your nose as you count to four, and hold your breath as you count to seven. Then exhale slowly through your mouth as you count to eight. This will relax your body and slow down your heart.

- **Keep your mind busy:** Repeatedly reciting a positive mantra can help with this (e.g., "I'm strong, and I'll get through this.") or counting the tiles on a wall. The idea is to give your mind something to focus on while your body slows down.

- **Use the "STOP protocol":** This involves telling your mind to stop and reframing your thinking. If, for example, you're scared by how hard your heart is pounding, say, "Stop," and remind yourself that you have a healthy heart that's working for your body.

- **Meditation:** This not only distracts your racing thoughts; it will also calm your mind and body. Guided meditation is great for this because you'll be taken through each step, and all you have to do is follow along. There are plenty of free guided meditations online—all it takes is a quick Google search.

- **Feel your feelings:** Don't avoid the emotions that are coming up for you. Allow yourself to experience them while reminding yourself that you're safe and the feeling will pass.

THE RESTORATIVE POWER OF RITUAL

Rituals provide us with a powerful mechanism for managing emotions and stress. If you were among the many people who scheduled a regular Friday night Zoom call with your family during the Covid lockdowns, you were engaging in a ritual that helped you to feel close to the people you couldn't see and process the stress and difficult emotions that many of us experienced during that time.

When we're dealing with loss, rituals can help us with our grief. The rituals we have within our families or with our partners help us to bond and feel close. They give us a sense of control during times when we feel like we have none, and this is very powerful. In a study conducted by researchers at Harvard Business School, it was found that people who performed rituals after a loss felt a little better after doing so and showed more emotional resilience. This was not so much to do with big rituals like funerals but more to do with small, personal acts, such as the routine washing of a passed loved one's car, the things that allowed for a sense of control and a framework through which to process the loss. I think this comes from the simple act of acknowledging your pain and accepting the need for a framework to deal with it. You have to own how you feel before you can get anywhere.

A ritual need not necessarily be repeated to count as a ritual. Burning the things that remind you of a relationship, as we discussed in the last chapter, for example, is a one-time thing, but it's still a ritual. What makes it powerful is that you decide it's a ritual and think of it as such—and it doesn't have to be practical. As long as it calms your mind and gives you a sense of control, it works. We can deliberately create new rituals to help us cope with something—and sometimes, it's those personal ones that work for us only because of our history that are the most powerful. We can tie this back to emotional alchemy—it's a way to help us cope with our circumstances and feel our emotions in a safe, structured way.

When I first moved back home, everything was new. I went from sharing meals every night to eating on my own. My work schedule was different because I was in another time zone, I had other people around me, and I had a completely new structure to my day. My working day started much later than I'd been used to, and I would put things in the way to fill the void in the morning. I'd keep myself busy with errands until work, and then I'd work until I was too tired to do anything else. I needed steadiness in order to deal with the massive changes I was going through. Gradually, as the pain that came with those changes started to lessen, I began building in my new self-care routines and discovering the immense value in those things. I'd been doing this a bit already, but it was like a Band-Aid to cover up the most painful moments until I was ready to start creating my new routines. This was all a lot for me to process, and packing my time with tasks helped to give me a sense of control, but so did the small rituals I built into my days—rituals I still use now. I listen to calming music in the morning and light a candle and an incense stick while I drink my coffee. It's peaceful and grounding and allows me a slow start to the day without beating myself up about not doing whatever it is I think I should be doing. It is an act of starting my day with control, and at a time when I felt untethered, this was hugely valuable to me.

Creating Your Own Rituals

The most powerful rituals are the personal ones, and I can't tell you what will work for you. Only you know that. However, I do have ideas you can use for inspiration, ideas that I've picked up from talking to other people or from looking for ways to process my own grief at different times. None of them account for the idiosyncratic things you might do that mean something to you because of your personal history; you'll find them as you need to, and many of them will emerge naturally.

- Light a candle at a particular time of the day.
- Light an incense stick.
- Build a memory scrapbook using mementos of your life together.
- Read a meaningful poem or say a prayer.
- Create a playlist of music that reminds you of the person you've lost.

- Watch your loved one's favorite movie.
- Plant a tree in their honor.
- Donate to a charity they supported.
- Carry a keepsake that you can take out and hold when you need to.
- Make the anniversary of a death into a holiday on which you celebrate their life.
- Create a place of memorial.
- Make a ceremony that involves making an offering of things they liked.
- Express gratitude to yourself for the lessons they taught you that you will carry forward.

Routines Help Too

The difference between a ritual and a routine is the intention. A ritual is a meaningful act with a particular purpose, while a routine is something you do out of necessity or as a way to organize your life. Rituals give us a sense of control and a way to understand and process our loss, but routine is a helpful tool for navigating grief, too.

Routines reduce the need for us to make decisions in the moment, and this, in turn, reduces the amount of stress we experience. Research shows that we display less self-control when we have more decisions to make, as well as getting more stressed as we make those decisions. When we have a particular structure to follow, we can end the day with a feeling of accomplishment rather than the sea of never-ending tasks that can loom over us when we're disorganized. A routine can help to counter feelings of loneliness and uncertainty by giving us a clear focus. If those routines also tick the self-care boxes, like the ones I've been building lately, then we also stand to gain benefits to our mental and physical health, and when we're feeling stronger in body and mind, those most difficult circumstances and emotions become easier to cope with. One of the reasons I find routines helpful is that they put my brain on autopilot. I don't have to think about making coffee in the morning; it's just something I do. That's a simple routine I have every day, and it's something I don't have to think about; I just move into action. We don't require willpower to do the things that are a part of our everyday routine, and that's one of the reasons making my self-care practices into one has been so helpful for me.

Creating a New Routine

This is all easier said than done, I know. Creating a routine from nothing can be daunting, and I can tell you I've had a few false starts as I've started building my new life. One skipped day in the early phases can set you back to square one—but if this happens, the trick is simply to pick yourself up and get started again. Bonus points if you can do that without hammering yourself for slipping up. If you're trying to build a new routine, try the following tactics:

- **Prioritize what you care about:** You can't do everything all at once, so start with what matters most to you. For me, it's self-care because that's something I'd been missing from my life for some time; for you, it might be a morning routine that gets you into the day feeling organized and steady, or it might be a specific exercise routine.

- **Keep track of your time:** If you look back at the day and don't know where it went, the chances are you've lost some time there that could have been better spent doing something specific. Keep a journal for a few weeks, tracking what you're doing with each hour of the day. Then, look back at it and see what you want to spend less time doing and where you could implement new routines. For me, this was in the morning before work: time I can use wisely but which easily disappears into doing very little (and passing very quickly) when I don't.

- **Eat the frog:** Yeah, that confused me too the first time I heard the expression. It comes from a saying that means if the first thing you do every day is to eat a live frog, nothing worse than that is going to happen to you for the rest of the day. In other words, if there's something you plan to do that you tend to put off, get that thing out of the way first. The rest of the day will seem easy in comparison, and you'll go into it with a sense of accomplishment.

- **Start gradually, and build up:** Planning to exercise every day if you're starting from nothing is going to be too much. Start with one or two days a week, and gradually add more in as you get stronger. Set yourself up for whatever it is you want to do the night before to make it easier on yourself. Maybe that's packing a gym bag or setting up a quiet space for meditation, or maybe it's making your week's lunches in advance or leaving your journal by the bed. Almost all routines can be made easier by planning in advance.
- **Tell someone your intention:** When you tell someone that you're trying to build a new routine, you're more likely to stick with it.

All of these points were relevant to me when I started building my self-care routines. I realized that looking after my health and well-being needed to be a priority, and I identified a time in the day I hadn't been using well in which to place those activities. I make them the way I start my day, both to set me up for everything ahead and to make sure I get out there and do it even if I don't feel like it. I started gradually with just short walks and not every day. As I got stronger and started feeling the benefits, my activities became longer and more frequent. I had told a couple of people about what I was doing, and that gave me an opportunity to reflect and share my successes, as well as giving me a source of encouragement and motivation.

From Routine to Ritual

Since the difference between a routine and a ritual has to do with attitude and intention, all it requires to turn one into the other is a change of perspective. Going for a walk during your lunch hour might start out as a routine you establish to make sure you're productive in the afternoon, but if you decide to view it as a way to break out of the confinements of the day and breathe in nature, then it can easily become a ritual. Each of the following routines could be a helpful way to find a structure and reduce the need for decision-making in the moment, but they could easily be turned into rituals if you find meaning and purpose in them, too.

Start-of-Day Routines

- **Get up early:** This has been associated with an increase in productivity and an energized mind, which leads to greater creativity. Some studies even suggest that early risers are happier and report a greater sense of well-being.
- **Make your bed:** I love this piece of advice from Navy Seal Admiral William H. McRaven. He says that by making your bed each morning, you automatically complete the first task of the day,

and that will lead to enough of a sense of pride to motivate yourself to do the next task. "Making your bed," he says, "will also reinforce the fact that the little things in life matter."

- **Eat a nutritious breakfast:** What you eat in the morning has an impact on your mood, energy levels, and productivity for the rest of the day. Steer clear of sugary foods, and focus on a balance of lean protein, healthy fat, complex carbohydrates, and fruits and vegetables. I confess I wasn't always great at this, but my go-to now is nut butter and banana on toast, and I've certainly felt the difference.

- **Use affirmations:** As we've discussed, these are a useful tool for overcoming negative self-talk, and they're particularly useful if you can ritualize them. The goal is to visualize the reality you want to achieve so that you begin to believe that you'll get there, and this will enable you to take the action needed to make it happen.

- **Exercise:** There's an abundance of information out there about the physical and mental health benefits of exercise, and we don't need to get into it all again here. Suffice to say, making it into a routine will make it non-negotiable, and if you're able to get to the point where you can see it as a ritual, it will become even more powerful.

End-of-Day

- **Prepare your goals for the next day:** This allows you to determine the most important tasks ahead of you before more gets thrown your way, and it means that your brain can start working on those things as you drift off to sleep.
- **Tidy up:** Just 10 minutes spent tidying up at the end of the day can significantly reduce the amount of stress you're exposed to in the morning. It can be very discouraging to come down to a sink full of dirty dishes or a coffee table strewn with books and papers. Make it easy for yourself by setting up a fresh canvas for the morning.
- **Prepare for the next morning:** I find it helpful to minimize the number of things I have to think about in the morning, and I try to make it easy for myself. Whether it's laying out tomorrow's clothes, packing a bag, or preparing your lunch, you'll have more energy for the things that truly matter if you get organized in advance, and you won't be kept awake worrying about whether you'll remember to do essential tasks.
- **Reflect on your achievements:** At the end of a long day, it's easy to lose sight of what we've accomplished, so building in a few minutes to celebrate small victories will give you a sense of perspective and motivate you to keep going the next day.

- **Clear your head:** If you've ever laid awake worrying about the tasks ahead of you at work the next day, you'll know that life can easily get in the way of a restful night's sleep. To allow your mind to shut down at the end of the day, practice meditation, journaling, reading, or watching an easy TV show to clear your mind.
- **Establish a bedtime routine:** I know very few adults who don't complain about their sleep quality, and most of us could do more to achieve better sleep hygiene. Create a routine by aiming to stick to the same sleep schedule, keep your bedroom cool and dark, and minimize the blue light emitted from your devices in the evenings.

➤ Tricks for Your Emotional Alchemy Bag

Implement one new routine by considering the advice in this chapter and following these steps:

1. Make a list of what's important to you.
2. Choose the one you want to make a priority.
3. Look at your schedule and identify the best time to do it.
4. Think about what you can do to make it automatic.
5. Set up a journal to reflect on your progress and how your new routine makes you feel day to day.

These routines and rituals help us to ride those surprising waves of grief, but it's important to acknowledge the emotions that come up for us. The goal is not to push those emotions away—we have to feel them as we move through the steps that will bring us to the other side and come back to peace. This is a way you can honor both yourself and your loved one. Let's take a look at how else we can do that.

7

UNITING NOW AND THEN: HONORING YOURSELF AS YOU HONOR THEM

"Being honest may not get you a lot of friends but it'll always get you the right ones."

— JOHN LENNON

I've always loved on other people's parents. It's a three-in-one way of honoring my own parents, honoring my needs, and supporting my friends. But I started doing this long before I lost my parents—it's something I've been doing ever since I was in third grade. I'd go over to a friend's house, they'd tell me their mother's name, and I'd call them "Mom" anyway. I don't know why I did this, but I know it came from a place of love. I think I wanted to see how other people lived and experience their family lives for myself. There was something about the stability there that I wanted. My parents were young, and although I was loved and cared for, that stability was something I missed. I was studying new territory and wanted to soak it up.

After I lost my parents, I adopted a few of my friends' parents. I called them "Mom" and "Dad." My friends were family to me, so their parents were family by extension, and I still show up for them now. One of my best friends lost his mom recently, and it was important to me that I showed up not only for him near the end but for her, too. A mother of two sons, she said to me once, "I have a daughter now," and I know she felt that I was part of the family as much as I did. She was a woman of many names, but to me, she will always be Ma. In her final months, we talked about her meeting my mom on the other side. It makes me smile to think of them together, at peace, and knowing my friend and I will always show up for each other when things get rough. The two of us are honoring them both by doing that, at the same time as taking care of ourselves and each other.

I talked a lot about honoring your grief and taking care of your own needs in the aftermath of a death in my first book, and I'd like to take this even further now to look at the relationship between those acts of honoring and moving toward peace and growing as a person. The way you honor loved ones lost—both still living and those who have passed away—is intertwined with how you honor yourself, and again, it's that balance between feeling the hard emotions and letting go of what hurts you.

TAKE WHAT'S GOOD AND IMPROVE ON IT

I no longer have my parents' limitations in life now that they're gone. I love who they were, and I'm grateful for everything they taught me, but honoring them doesn't have to mean doing everything the way they did it—in fact, to honor them is to listen to what they taught me and improve on it for myself. We can always do better. This can be done in small ways, like tweaking a recipe to add depth to the flavor, or in larger ways, like taking a viewpoint you respect and expanding it to include more nuance than they were able to see.

Sometimes, we hold on to habits or behaviors simply because they were those of our loved ones, without questioning whether they serve us in the life we have now. I realized not long ago, for example, that I was still cutting pills in half because that's what my mom did to save money—that's not something I need to do in my current life, yet I've been doing it out of habit because it's what she did. Some things, on the other hand, still serve us. For example, my mom taught me how to fold laundry in a particular way, and that's something I not only still do; it's something I pass on to others. That still serves me, and it's a skill I can keep, but it's worth questioning why we do things a certain way and whether it still makes sense for us.

There's a phenomenon known as the "social proximity effect," which sees us mirroring the habits of those with whom we spend the most time. That's great if those are good habits, but not so much if those habits are harmful or stand in the way of us becoming our best selves. Research shows, for example, that children are four times more likely to become regular smokers if their caregivers smoke. It's important to be mindful of the social proximity effect because it can so strongly influence our perspective and behavior. Not only are we affected by the behaviors and habits of those around us, but their viewpoints become ours, too. We want to be sure that we're only adopting habits that support us on our own path rather than getting swayed by those who take us in the opposite direction. We can turn the social proximity effect to our advantage, too, deliberately surrounding ourselves with people who have habits and behaviors we'd like to have ourselves. It's the opposite of walking away from people who you recognize aren't good for you—it's walking toward those who you can see are.

This segues into its other side—we learn things from everyone who enters our life in any capacity. Sometimes, when we're grieving, there's a temptation to turn our backs on the lessons or skills we've learned from people we've lost, but we can't omit things just because the people who showed us them aren't there anymore. We have to bring it all in. That is honoring the people we've lost—even those who still live but from whom we've chosen to part ways—and it's honoring ourselves. Every single one of those lessons helped us to grow and become who we are today. We can't move forward authentically by turning our backs on those things and denying who we are. Everyone we've ever had a relationship with leaves their mark on us—all those experiences are part of us, and it serves both ourselves and our future relationships best when we can honor that.

HONORING YOURSELF AS YOU MOVE FORWARD

Part of the healing process involves recognizing that honoring yourself is important and doesn't take anything away from how much you love and miss those who are gone. In the early stages of grief, it's common to feel guilty about doing anything to move forward or look for joy in life, but you're still here. You owe it to yourself and to everyone you love to find a way forward. Honoring yourself *is* honoring the people you've lost, and there's comfort to be found in knowing that they would be proud of the decisions you're making for yourself.

Treat Yourself With Honesty

The word "honesty" comes from the Latin word *honestus*, meaning "regarded with honor," so it stands to reason that a big part of honoring yourself is being honest ... and that means listening to yourself. This isn't always easy to do, and when the real you is saying something that doesn't align with the life you've chosen, it's very tempting to do everything you can to ignore it. If you have trouble with tuning into what your feelings are saying to you, journaling is a good call. It allows you to write out what you need to and then look back on it with a more objective perspective, and it can bring your hidden feelings to the surface. I've gotten to the point that my feelings were so loud I couldn't ignore them anymore, but not before a considerable amount of time burying them and keeping myself as busy as possible so I didn't have to think about them. I'm better at listening to myself now, but it takes work and a willingness to get real with yourself in a way that isn't always comfortable.

Give Yourself Time

Some parts of listening to yourself are easier than others. It's not always easy to treat yourself with the compassion you deserve when you're exhausted, but it's usually easier to know that you're worn out than it is to know how you feel about a complex dynamic in your life. The hard part is honoring your need to take some time out to wind down and do something that makes you feel good. Part of the trick to that for me was making self-care part of my routine and sticking with it for long enough to now be able to say, "I need a sauna," or to book a massage. When we don't give ourselves time to re-energize, we can't give our best to our work, to our relationships, or to ourselves. We end up wiped out, either emotionally or physically, and if the reason we were reluctant to take time out in the first place was that we didn't want to let anyone down, we're missing the best chance we had to make sure that didn't happen.

We've all been guilty of putting ourselves at the bottom of the list. You need to make sure your responsibilities at work are met, do the laundry, pack lunches for the family, and cook dinner. Then, if you get time, maybe you can have an hour for yourself. If you need that hour to yourself, then that should be a priority. As long as it's not, something new will vie for your attention every time. Listen to what each part of you—heart, mind, and body—needs, and make sure you meet their requests. If you're tired, rest; if you're hungry, eat; if you need an hour to not be social, give yourself time alone. You can only give yourself to everything else once you have a solid foundation to work from, and to do that, you must listen to your own needs.

Set Boundaries

Boundary setting is a skill, and if you're not used to it, it can feel uncomfortable to begin with, but I promise you, it pays off. Start with the small things: turn off your phone notifications when you're not working or if you need some time to yourself. I've personally found that my stress levels have gone down enormously since I started doing this, and I know I won't miss anything I want to see because I always check my personal messages when I'm ready. Turn down requests that ask for more of you than you're able to give. The more you do this, the more you'll know, understand, and appreciate yourself and your limitations. If your friend wants to hang out at the last minute and you planned an evening alone that you don't want to give up, allow yourself to say no and stand up for what you need. The older I get, the more I realize that nearly everyone wants to do this sometimes, and a true friend will only meet you with understanding—even if they have to put you through a bit of pleading to get there. Setting boundaries in these small day-to-day situations will help you practice the skill enough that when it comes to setting bigger boundaries, like not tolerating certain kinds of behavior, you'll be better equipped to handle the task.

Get the Support Balance Right

We've talked about surrounding yourself with positive people who love you as you are, but it's worth mentioning again because it's an important part of honoring yourself. If someone is constantly making you feel small or putting you down, you owe it to yourself to take a step back from the situation. Spending too much time in this environment sucks away your energy, and it can leave you with little enthusiasm or creativity. Focus on spending your time with people who support you and make you feel safe to be who you really are. These are the people you should feel comfortable asking for support from and talking through your decisions with. This isn't to say that you should take their advice as gospel—it's equally important that when it comes down to it, you make your own decisions, using their advice only as an additional perspective to draw on.

Give Yourself Growing Space

You always need the space to allow yourself to grow in your own direction, even within a healthy relationship. In a romantic relationship, it's actually better, not only for your sake as an individual but for the growth of your relationship as a unit, if you each have room to pursue your own interests. We should all be on a continuous journey of development, and every relationship in your life should allow for this and be given the chance to benefit from each person's individual growth.

Say the Thing

How many times have you told someone you were okay, knowing you're not really okay at all? We're programmed to be polite and not ruffle any feathers, and sometimes, it seems like not speaking up is the easy way out. What I've learned, though, is that even when it seems like the easy route, it's harder in the long run. That feeling, whatever it is, sits inside you and brews. You end up harboring resentment, and in some cases, that comes out in a far more volatile way further down the line. We can't expect people to know what we need if we don't communicate it, no matter how well they know us. When we don't speak up for ourselves, we run into a stalemate situation, and we can't move forward. Saying the thing, no matter how uncomfortable it feels at the time, involves one potentially difficult conversation; keeping it to yourself could mean months of anxiety and discomfort. Plus, it's often the case that it's nowhere near as difficult as you fear, and your unease is immediately pacified when you have that conversation—and it doesn't need to be hostile or aggressive. You're in control, and you can approach it gently and kindly while still standing up for what you need.

This becomes much easier when you're able to be authentically you. It's always okay to speak up for yourself. You do yourself a disservice when you tell someone you're fine when you're not. The goal is not simply to survive; it's to thrive. And to do that means accepting who you are and recognizing that who you are is enough.

This has nothing to do with your circumstances or your success—it's about your attitude and behavior. When you're true to yourself, you have the power to create a life in which you can thrive. It starts within you, but sometimes that means speaking up outside of you, and only when you do that can you be sure you're being true to yourself in all situations. Doing something different from what's expected of you takes courage, and that includes saying the thing, but you're worth every ounce of that courage.

HONORING PAST RELATIONSHIPS

Our relationships reflect the parts of us that we truly want to be known. They show us our beliefs about who we are, and they can tell us a lot about the way we treat ourselves. No matter whether that relationship was healthy or destructive, it can show us a pathway back to ourselves, illustrating what we want and what we need if we're to find the fulfillment we seek. This applies to all relationships, to an extent, but none so much as a romantic relationship.

You're in Charge of Your Experience

Is it possible to turn a breakup into a positive experience? I believe it is, but that doesn't mean you get to sidestep the pain of your relationship ending. On the contrary, you have to feel it all. It starts with validating your pain and accepting that you need to grieve for what has been lost. Doing this may seem like the most painful way you could handle it, but, in fact, it gives you much more ownership and will allow you to move through the hurt more quickly —without it sneaking up on you when you're trying to ignore it.

Make a conscious decision to remember what hurts you about not being in that relationship anymore. It's a part of what made you who you are today, and no matter how right the decision was to end it (whoever made the decision), it's okay to feel sad about it. Making a conscious decision to sit with your pain in this way is known as "intentional grieving." If you're struggling with this, try giving yourself a framework. Think of three memories you have in which you recall feeling truly happy with the other person. Don't brush them aside or try to find a dark side to them; honor the fact that you chose that person and you loved them. Let those happy memories stay in your past as positive experiences. There's no reason you can't continue to validate them just because your relationship changed or ended completely.

The next part you have to handle is the reality of being on your own, and trust me, I know how hard this is. But working out what makes you happy on your own sets you up to be the best version of yourself, not only in your future relationships but in all the other relationships you still have. You had plans, a dream for the future, and when all that is ripped out from under you, it can leave you feeling lost and anxious. Healing begins with you, and that means channeling any negative energy you're feeling in a positive way—the alternative is that it sits inside you, stewing and making you feel worse until, eventually, it bubbles over. What this looks like is different for everyone, but finding a way to physically release some of that energy can help make sense of your emotions. Perhaps exercise is the best option for you, or maybe it's journaling. Either way, it's a physical act that will allow you to channel that energy outside of yourself.

Moving Forward

You can only control your own actions, so it may be that you have less say in how your relationship ends than you'd like. It may also be the case that you're already past the breakup stage, and it's too late to do anything about the way it ended. But if you're currently in the process of separation or you're making the difficult decision to end a relationship—and if the other person is onside—it is possible to part ways on good terms. This doesn't mean that you have to be best friends—or even friends at all. It may be that you never speak again, but you can still do this in a civil way that won't leave either of you with any bitterness.

As you move forward, take time to deal with your loss—whether you're grieving the end of a dream or the loss of a specific person being in your life, you're going through significant change, and it's important to honor yourself in that process. That means making an effort to enjoy your life, too. There will be days that are more difficult than others—days where you barely recognize your life—but there's joy to be found in every one of those days if you commit yourself to finding it.

Allow yourself to feel the grief and look at the places in your relationship where you wanted something to change. What does that tell you about yourself and what you need in order to be happy and fulfilled? You can use this relationship and your experience of it ending to fuel your inner growth. If there are moments where you wish your partner had acted differently, what does that tell you about your own needs? How can you use that to help you love yourself better? That relationship has stories to tell you about your own need for healing. It tells you more about what you need from a partner and from yourself. And, if you're willing to see it, it can bring hope for the kind of relationships you can attract in the future. Perhaps you'll never be with someone with this exact quality that you miss again; perhaps you'll never be in a relationship with exactly the same dynamic; perhaps you'll never feel this exact same way again… But there are many ways to love and be loved, and you can attract a better version now that you know more about yourself and your needs. You attracted this relationship into your life, and you felt love. That means you have the power to do those things again.

Use your relationship as a tool to tap into your true self. When we're in a romantic relationship, we understand how to feel a particular way because of the other person— but we have that within ourselves, and your relationship has shown you that it's there inside you. You have a chance to nurture that and, eventually, share it with someone else. Allow yourself to appreciate the beauty of your relationship as it was, and reflect on the darker parts as symbols of what you fear. The beauty is the love within you that you want to receive and to give back; the darker parts show you what you've shut down in yourself or what you're afraid of. These are the parts of you where love is desperate to shine through, but until you open it back up, it remains in the shadows.

None of this is to say that leaving a relationship is easy, whether you've chosen it or not. But there is an opportunity here for learning and growth, and what better legacy for a relationship to have? To embrace that opportunity is to honor the relationship. It's to say, "I'm thankful for what I had, I'm thankful for what it taught me, and now I'm ready to move forward."

HONORING LOVED ONES WHO HAVE PASSED

I'm going to touch on this only lightly since we've already looked at the importance of rituals. However, honoring those who have passed away is a significant part of healing, and it ties in so deeply with how we honor ourselves that it's important to bring it back here.

Live for Them

Even the smallest things seem meaningless when you lose someone you love. What's the point of going to work? Why does it matter if that presentation ticks all the boxes that seemed so important at the last meeting? This does become easier, and no one expects you to find your way through immediately. But the way out of the darkness is to find those little lights along the path—those small reasons there are to live on for the person you've lost. And they *are* small reasons. It's those seemingly inconsequential moments that add up to a whole life—a life that the person you've lost would have wanted you to live. It's important to allow yourself the time to grieve, but it's important to live, too. I think it's remembering that it's what they would want that's the most helpful thing in forcing yourself to keep going in the darkest moments. If they could see you now, in this moment, how would they feel? What could you do to make them happier? Make your bed … Start with that. As Admiral McRaven himself said, "And if by chance you have a miserable day, you will come home to a bed that is made … And a made bed gives you encouragement that tomorrow will be better." (McRaven 2014)

Live for Others

Grieving is an incredibly isolating experience. We know on paper that everyone goes through this, often multiple times in their life, yet when we're in it, it's hard to accept that anyone could possibly know what we're going through. Everyone's experience is unique; everyone is affected differently by their losses, but nearly everyone knows something of grief—not least the people around you who have also lost someone. Maybe you lost your sister, but her best friend also lost her greatest support … your aunt lost her niece … your brother lost his sister … They're grieving, too. There's some purpose to be found in recognizing that we can support each other through loss. Being strong for the sake of another person gives you a purpose and an opportunity to talk about all the good memories you share. There's joy to be found here—especially if you find yourselves exchanging stories one or other of you didn't know.

Keep Their Legacy Alive

A legacy can live forever if we enable it to do so. Think about what was important to your loved one and how you can use that knowledge to honor them. Perhaps it's holding a fundraiser, or maybe it's arranging for a memorial to be placed in their favorite park. Maybe it's writing a song or hosting an event. All of these things can provide inspiration and hope to other people and keep your loved one's legacy alive. The enigmatic street artist Banksy is thought to have said, "They say you die twice. One time when you stop breathing, and a second time, a bit later on, when somebody says your name for the last time." Legacies live on—as long as we keep someone's memory alive, as long as we keep on telling stories and passing the memories down the generations, as long as that name continues to be spoken, they continue to live. My mom lives in every story I tell about her. I keep her legacy alive through writing and using my experiences to help others.

➤ Tricks for Your Emotional Alchemy Bag

Honoring yourself as you heal requires you to recognize your pain so that you can truly address it … and that brings us back to radical acceptance. I know how tough this is in the beginning, but it's a skill, and the best way to perfect any skill is to practice it. Start by listing some things you can radically accept—one small, one medium, and one big. Since we're practicing the skill here, move away from the area in which you're currently healing. Being able to identify where radical acceptance is needed will be key to using it for the hardest issues.

E.g., Small—Someone jumped in line in front of me at the store.
Medium—I burned dinner.
Big—I didn't get the position I applied for.

When the goal is peace, we have to be willing to get uncomfortable. We have to be prepared to feel those difficult emotions in order to honor ourselves and our loved ones and grow from our experiences. And that brings us to what, ultimately, we're all searching for within our healing journeys: peace and fulfillment.

8

THE MISSING PEACE: WORKING TOWARD THE FUTURE WE WANT

"No one can bring you peace but yourself."

— RALPH WALDO EMERSON

I have clawed for every ounce of peace I have. Some days, I claw harder to maintain it than others, pulling out everything in the bag of tricks. I told you about Father's Day creeping up on me and blindsiding me with emotion. This was one of those days. I hadn't kept track of the date, and I wasn't prepared for the well of emotion I would feel. I missed my dad, and my guard was down. I was missing other people who were no longer in my life, and I was worrying about the ones who were. I had to systematically work through every trick I knew to level myself out, and finding the strength to do the things I knew would help me was hard. I made myself get out of bed, even though everything in me was pulling me back; I made myself eat; I did breathing exercises; I made myself get out of the house and to the sauna; I talked to someone I love. Piece by piece, I started to feel myself again through the fog. It was slow, and it took all day, but by the end of the day, my auntie and I were cracking my dad's favorite beer and celebrating his memory. I can't say I felt completely at peace, but I could feel the shape of it. I knew it was waiting for me. I just had to allow myself to feel the pain and do everything I knew I could do to help myself feel better.

SELF-REFLECTION AS A GATEWAY TO PEACE

Self-reflection allows us to move from experiencing to understanding. It encourages self-awareness and an increased level of consciousness about our actions, and that's important because it helps us to know what peace means to us and what we need to do to achieve it. When we practice self-reflection, we develop our "inner witness" —that is to say, we develop our ability to look at our thoughts and emotions from a slightly removed perspective. We become able to observe ourselves with curiosity and interest, becoming aware of the sensations in our bodies and how our thoughts and emotions affect us. From here, we can ask ourselves why certain thoughts are coming up and what deeper feelings may be below the surface. This is an essential skill to practice if we're to achieve personal growth. Without it, we're likely to be reactive, not just to each other, but to ourselves. It enables us to choose healthier responses and move away from behaviors that aren't serving us. When we're able to reflect on our successes, we build resilience, which, in turn, helps us to process difficult experiences. Ultimately, self-reflection is an act of self-care … but it needs to be used with caution. If it becomes obsessive, it can easily become self-judgment, and if it's turning into an invitation for your inner critic to jump out of its box, then it's not helpful. Self-reflection should be a tool that guides you toward positive change and better ways of honoring yourself.

Practicing Self-Reflection

As with most things, the key to making self-reflection work for you is to do it with intention. Journaling is a helpful tool for this. Decide on the period you want to reflect on, whether that's the last day or the last year, consider what happened during that time, and write down the highs and lows. If you're struggling to get the juices flowing, these prompt questions may help you unlock what you need to:

- Were there any big milestones?
- Did you travel?
- What changes did you experience at work or in your relationships?
- What were the highs and lows, and do you notice any patterns?

- Did your highs always involve the same people or activities? How about the lows?

When you think about the low points, consider whether they were within your control. If the answer is yes, your task is to think about what you could do differently if the situation were to arise again. If the answer is no, it's time to let it go and consider how you can make peace with it. Think about your overall experience of the time period you're looking at. How did you feel in your mind, body, and soul? Did you experience joy? Were you fulfilled by your work? Did you feel positive about your relationships? Write down how you feel about this now. This is reflecting on your self-reflection, and it will deepen your understanding of and connection with yourself.

As you become more skilled at this process, you may find it helpful to put a few minutes aside at the end of each week to deliberately reflect on the week behind you. It can also be helpful to do this at the end of each year. In reflections that look back over longer periods, it may be helpful to ask yourself these questions:

- What would I like to change about my circumstances or behaviors? How could I achieve this?
- What things in my life do I want more of, and what do I want to see less of?
- Where can I see myself in five years?

- How could I be a better partner/friend/parent/colleague?
- What are my strengths and weaknesses?
- What do I feel passionate about?
- What do I have to be grateful for?
- Do I have any regrets? What can I do to let go of them?
- Are there any limiting beliefs or fears holding me back from achieving my goals?

When you're looking at areas to change or improve, start small. The goal of being a better friend is probably overwhelming, and when you look at it like that, it will be impossible to know where to start. Instead, break it down and tackle one thing at a time. Perhaps you'll call your friends more often, or perhaps you're going to work on being a better listener. As you continue the process of self-reflection, you can assess what's working and what isn't and add more goals as you meet others.

SLOWING DOWN

Happiness is an inside job. It starts with you … and for me, slowing down has been key. Slowing down is a helpful tool for letting go of the need to control everything. Think of a plant growing... When you plant a seed, growth begins at the root—a process we can't see but that we trust is happening. The same is true for you—you don't have to be constantly "on" to be making progress.

Not every growth is visible. When we slow down, we have an opportunity to gain perspective and become more present in the moment. When we're rushing, it's all too easy to let our thoughts and worries take over—and if you've made rushing into a habit, it's worth questioning why that might be. There's a chance you're trying to fill your time so you don't have to sit with what you're really feeling. This can serve to a point—filling my mornings with tasks when I first moved back home was helpful to me finding stability, but there came a time when I had to slow down and be with myself.

Being slow is a lesson in patience. There are times when we have no choice but to wait, and if we've already taught ourselves the art of slowing down, we can draw on that when we need to. It gives us a chance to reflect and be grateful for where we are now, acknowledging the small achievements that are taking us to where we want to be. As we do this, we build up our resilience. We learn endurance, persistence, and the willingness to keep going. There's a risk, when we're rushing, that whatever our goal is takes on a life of its own. We become obsessed and live for that one thing, and that comes with two further risks: one, that once that goal is met or becomes unattainable, we've lost sight of what we truly need to feel at peace; and two, that life passes us by. For me, it's all about the little things, and when I'm going fast, I barely have a chance to notice them … I forget to pay attention to the things that make me happy and bring me peace. I've been there, and I don't want to go back. For me, slowing down is vital.

When we're rushing through life, there's a risk that we'll follow a path that isn't meant for us. Perhaps it's a path laid by someone else, or maybe it's just the easiest or most obvious. But when we slow down, we can be more intentional in our decision-making and choose the path most suited to our needs and goals. Perhaps we can do more when we're fast, but that doesn't mean we're doing what's best. If we slow down, we don't only produce better quality; we also experience higher quality. What's more, it's actually sustainable. Live your life at 100 miles an hour, and you're going to burn out. You need downtime and the space to reflect and take care of yourself.

What Does Slowing Down Look Like?

When you're used to going fast, slowing down can be very difficult to achieve. You may feel at a loss when you're suddenly faced with a free hour, or you may feel guilty about all the things you think you should be doing. If slowing down is something you struggle with, try these approaches:

- **Be selective about your commitments:** Turn down the things you have neither the time nor energy for, and say no to anything that doesn't fit with your values.

- **Engage in mindfulness:** Pay attention to your surroundings and try to be in the moment more, letting go of worries about things that have already happened or what might happen in the future.
- **Approach tasks mindfully:** Aim to stay focused on exactly what you're doing rather than having half your mind on the next job.
- **Incorporate breaks into your day:** They don't have to be long—even five minutes outside or a few deep breaths is enough to reset you sometimes.
- **Make time for self-care:** Go for a walk, meditate, or book yourself in for a massage. Take the time to do whatever it is that makes you feel good.
- **Arrange to do the things that make you happy:** Reading, pursuing an interest, or spending time with people you love are all valuable ways to slow down.
- **Try to simplify your routine:** Write to-do lists and keep your work and living spaces tidy so you don't constantly have to be decluttering as you go.
- **Incorporate slowness into all areas of your life:** Eat more slowly, savoring the food and paying attention to its flavors and textures; approach communication slowly, listening attentively and explaining your point fully; take your time when you're making decisions—you'll probably find that

you make better ones when you approach them slowly and deliberately.

MAKING PEACE WITH YOURSELF

Consciously making an effort to slow down made it much clearer to me what I was missing and what I was searching for. My missing piece was … peace. Peace is not found in a single moment but somewhere deep within us, and it's when everything seems to be going fast and without our control that we need it the most. We need it to make positive changes and keep our mental health intact along the way. But it's not our circumstances that give us that peace—it's ourselves within those circumstances. Psychotherapist Ashley Davis Bush says that within each one of us, there is a calm awareness, "as if we have a deep reservoir of peacefulness and serenity inside us. What we have to learn to do is tap into it." I feel like I found that through my ketamine treatments—that sense of being in the pocket observing everything happening around me is something I've been able to take forward. That pocket is a metaphor for my inner peace—which isn't to say that I feel it all the time; that's a work in progress. But I recognize it now, and I understand how important it is to me. When I tune in, I can get back into that pocket, knowing that I'm safe, I'm loved, and I know myself.

Tapping Into Your Reservoir of Peace

When we're healing or we're fighting hard to change our circumstances, that sense of peace feels like it's far away. There have been times when it has seemed that if I even knew that peace came from within, I have forgotten it, and there have been times when my circumstances have kept it hidden from me. So, how can you tap into that reservoir during the hardest times?

Breathing has always been a good fallback for me. Whenever I feel like I'm going fast and I need to bring myself back to peace, I take a few deep breaths. It's a technique used in meditation and yoga to help move you out of a particular state of mind, and there are many ways to approach it. I like box breathing because it has simple rules, and it's easy to recall when everything's racing—It's made up of four simple steps, each lasting for four seconds. Breathe in through your nose; hold your breath; exhale through your mouth; hold your breath … and repeat until you feel the difference in your mind and body. What you're doing is stimulating your parasympathetic nervous system, triggering your body to deliver a relaxation response.

Gratitude helps me a lot, too. I remind myself that I'm safe; I remind myself that I'm loved. Focusing on the thoughts of the people I love and who love me helps me to reduce my panic response, and I'm able to access the knowledge that this moment won't last forever.

Many people also find it helpful to visualize a place that makes them happy. For me, that's the ocean, and when I'm able to visualize it clearly, it helps to calm me. It need not even be a place—it could be a person or a pet. Try to see all the details—everything from the smells to the sounds and textures. The more vivid a memory you can tap into, the more you can trick your body into thinking you're really there, and the more likely you are to relax.

Once you're calm enough to do so, pay attention to the story you're telling yourself. Is it really true? Allow yourself to feel the hard emotions, but recognize what's happening, and refrain from creating narratives based on assumptions.

These are all good techniques for handling a specific moment in which peace seems like a faraway goal, but it's something we need to cultivate all the time to make it easier to access when we need it. I think it starts with knowing who you want to be. What qualities do you want to nurture in yourself? Would you like to be more patient, kinder, more tolerant? What values do you want to stand by? When you're clear on these elements, it gives you grounding and a framework through which to understand yourself, and that makes it much easier to pinpoint that reservoir. If you find yourself not acting within that framework in response to a tough situation, don't beat yourself up about it. If you make a mistake, do the next right thing. Maybe you could have handled that one conversation better, but you can't do anything about that now. What you can do is reach out and make it right. That takes strength and courage, and, as someone who's had to do this a number of times, I can tell you there's immense peace and growth in it. It's not easy to avoid hammering yourself for those mistakes, I know, but you'll make yourself feel worse if you do. You can be imperfect and still make progress—in fact, that's the whole package of being human.

I've been on a journey of patience over the last few years, and it's unlocked another avenue to peace for me. Perhaps other people around you don't live the way you choose to, but that's for them to live with. As long as you respond to them in a way that gives you peace of mind, you're doing everything you need to do for your own peace. Whether you ultimately need to walk away or you simply need to work around strict boundaries with that person, you can still come from a loving place and control your response to them. Seeking to understand is helpful here, too. As you learn to let go and forgive, you set yourself free. Compassion puts positivity out into the world, and you can model how you want it to look, even if the other person isn't responding how you would have liked them to. It will probably have more effect than you realize, and you might be surprised at what comes back to you—sometimes, it's more than you were able to get when you were fighting for it.

Forgiveness is something you should extend to yourself, too. Forgive yourself for those small mistakes, and move on rather than get stuck on them. Growth requires movement, and getting stuck in a place of regret keeps you from moving forward. Be kind to yourself when you make those mistakes—and even when you don't. However you're feeling is okay, and you'll move through it. Being kind to yourself also means paying attention to your best qualities rather than dismissing them. Acknowledge the good things about yourself, and it becomes much easier to work on the areas you'd like to improve. This means accepting compliments, too, and I know that's not easy. I've felt uncomfortable and awkward when I've been complimented before, and I've dismissed kind words before I've truly taken them in and appreciated what they meant. I'm better at this now, and it helps me to see the good in myself. Acknowledge what's being said, and thank the other person for their compliment—there's immense freedom in that. Ultimately, all of this is feeding your ability to validate yourself, and that's a real gateway to tapping into that inner peace. Notice your progress, acknowledge what you've done well, and take pride in that. You'll find that a taste of that peace isn't so far away.

Dealing With Other People

Accepting and being proud of who you are doesn't mean there isn't still room for growth. We can always be better—and that's an exciting part of the journey. Surrounding yourself with people who love you and accept you for who you are is important, but there's more to consider here when it comes to people.

People are mirrors: we see ourselves in them. Why is it that you don't like a particular quality in someone? Is it reminding you of something you don't like in yourself? If so, what can you do about that? Equally, if there's something you see in someone else that you view as positive and that speaks to you, the chances are you're seeing a quality you have yourself. Own that, and be proud of it. Reflecting on these notices is an opportunity for growth—and growth will always bring you closer to your goals.

It's worth noting, however, that not everyone will understand as you do this work on yourself. People don't always want to be this clear and honest with themselves, and when you are, it can be intimidating for them, and they don't know how to react. For me, the way to deal with this is to come back to that piece about understanding. Consider yourself at other times in your life and how you would have reacted then. That's a place you respect and understand, and you can meet them there, no matter how at odds your journeys seem to be now.

As you find your peace, you may come up against surprising reactions from other people. Perhaps it unsettles them, or perhaps you've had to put boundaries in place to protect it. Maybe they need some time to get used to a more peaceful version of you, one that isn't as likely to come in hot, or maybe they simply want that peace for themselves. Let that roll off your back. That has more to do with them than it does to do with you, and engaging with it will only take you further from your peace.

➤ Tricks for Your Emotional Alchemy Bag

If you're considering making changes to move you toward what you truly want, try asking yourself these self-reflection questions:

Why do I want this?
What will I gain from it?
What will it require me to let go of?
What would life be like if I did nothing?
What will life be like if I succeed?

My journey since I moved away from my old life has been a story of getting back to basics. It's been about looking at what I really want versus what I thought I wanted and stripping away everything that has stood in my way and prevented me from cultivating the feeling I craved. It's been about slowing down and finding my peace.

THE EMOTIONAL ALCHEMIST

"The human heart has a way of making itself large again even after it's been broken into a million pieces"

— ROBERT JAMES WALLER

Healing is an ongoing process. I still have days that knock me for six, days that I feel all the pain as if it were fresh. But I'm in a vastly different place than I was when I first moved away from Arizona. Reflection has been important for me in that journey—recognizing what really makes me happy and looking at what I can do to bring more of those things into my life. I feel a greater sense of peace now, and I'm able to access that pocket I first found in my ketamine treatments—that sense of peace that comes from within me. Being at peace is the most important thing. When I'm at peace with myself, I can truly appreciate what I have, clearly see what I want, and show up for the people I love in the best way I possibly can.

Healing requires emotional alchemy. It requires you to take that pain, own it, feel it, and listen to what it can teach you so you can transform it into something you can use to create the life you want: a life that provides you with peace. That's done by prioritizing what you need to keep you well and in touch with yourself and your goals. It's done through honoring yourself and your loved ones. It's done through reflection. And it hurts... but the rewards are immense. Stick with it, and you'll become an emotional alchemist. You'll be more resilient and better prepared to handle the next painful thing that comes your way. So allow yourself to feel the things, say the things, and honor yourself. You deserve that.

Healing is a journey, and it never truly ends. Embrace the path, take it one step at a time, and appreciate the joy you find along the way. Every single piece of it is taking you further ... and now, in this moment, you're right where you need to be.

AN INVITATION

My journey as an emotional alchemist involves sharing what I've learned and getting raw to help others. Your feedback is vital to that process.

By sharing your honest opinion of this book and, if you're comfortable with it, something about your own healing journey, you'll not only show new readers where they can find the support they're looking for; you'll help me improve my work, too.

Thank you so much for your input. I wish you great success and joy as you head forward on your path.

For those who have dared to dream their dream, for those who encourage the dreamers, and for those who clap silently with tears in their eyes.

BIBLIOGRAPHY

Attard, A. (2020, November 4). *Repressing emotions: 10 ways to reduce emotional avoidance.* PositivePsychology.Com. https://positivepsychology.com/repress-emotions/

Ackerman, C. E. (2019, April 27). *What are positive and negative emotions and do we need both?* PositivePsychology.Com. https://positivepsychology.com/positive-negative-emotions/

Akpan, N. (2019, February 14). *Why that one song will always remind you of your ex.* PBS NewsHour. https://www.pbs.org/newshour/science/why-that-song-will-always-remind-you-of-your-ex

Altrogge, S. (n.d.). *12 morning and evening routines that will set up each day for success.* Zapier. https://zapier.com/blog/daily-routines

Anderson, B. (2014, February 17). *14 mantras to help you build positive self-talk.* Mindbodygreen. https://www.mindbodygreen.com/articles/mantras-to-build-positive-self-talk

Andonian, N. (2022, August 19). *13 sauna benefits that'll have you ready to feel the heat.* GoodRx Health. https://www.goodrx.com/well-being/alternative-treatments/sauna-benefits

Arsdale, H. V. (2017, March 22). *What to do with sentimental items (and how to store them).* Elbow Room. https://www.clutter.com/blog/posts/sentimental-items

Banksy quotes (Author of wall and piece). (n.d.). https://www.goodreads.com/author/quotes/28811.Banksy

Bengtson, M. (2022, November 28). *12 reasons to return to our roots.* https://drmichellebengtson.com/12-reasons-to-return-to-our-roots

Bennett, T. (2018, June 7). *How is therapy beneficial? 5 people explain how therapy helped them heal, improve relationships, manage their emotions, and more.* Thriveworks. https://thriveworks.com/blog/therapy-beneficial-people-weigh-in-experiences

Berinato, S. (2020, April 2). *The restorative power of ritual.* Harvard

Business Review. https://hbr.org/2020/04/the-restorative-power-of-ritual

Bern, K. (2017, October 11). *Why leaving people behind as we grow is essential.* Kat Bern. https://katbern.com/leaving-people-behind-grow-essential

Beutell, C. (2022, December). *Health benefits of having a routine.* Northwestern Medicine. https://www.nm.org/healthbeat/healthy-tips/health-benefits-of-having-a-routine

Brown, M. (2015, October 4). *What radical acceptance really means.* Psych Central. https://psychcentral.com/blog/what-it-really-means-to-practice-radical-acceptance

Burgess, L. (2017, October 7). *8 benefits of crying: Why do we cry, and when to seek support.* https://www.medicalnewstoday.com/articles/319631

Ciszewski, K. (2020, September 11). *5 reasons grief comes in waves (and how to deal with it).* https://www.facebook.com/kasiatherapy/posts/new-blog-post-5-reasons-grief-comes-in-waves-grief-trauma-depression-anxiety-the/758565221381315/?locale=ms_MY

Clark, A. H. (2023, January 18). *6 ways grief can make you wonder if you'll ever be ok.* Clark Psychology Group. https://aliciaclarkpsyd.com/6-ways-grief-can-make-wonder-youll-ever-ok

Community service quotes. (n.d.). Lycoming College. https://www.lycoming.edu/community-service/community-service-quotes.aspx

Compitus, K. (2020, October 20). *12 radical acceptance worksheets for your dbt sessions.* PositivePsychology.Com. https://positivepsychology.com/radical-acceptance-worksheets

Daniels, J. K., & Vermetten, E. (2016). *Odor-induced recall of emotional memories in PTSD—Review and new paradigm for research.* Experimental Neurology, 284, 168–180. https://doi.org/10.1016/j.expneurol.2016.08.001

Druck, K. (2021, January 23). *Closure is a myth. Healing is a lifelong process.* Dr Ken Druck. https://www.kendruck.com/blog/closure-is-a-myth-healing-is-a-lifelong-process

Focus on the Present for Radical Acceptance. (n.d.). Positive Psychology. https://positive.b-cdn.net/wp-content/uploads/2020/10/Focus-on-the-Present-for-Radical-Acceptance.pdf

GoLeanSixSigma.com. (2017, February 24). https://goleansixsigma. com/everything-seem-going-remember-airplane-takes-off-wind-not/

Grohl, D. (2021). *The Storyteller: Tales of Life and Music* (1st edition 5). Simon & Schuster UK.

Habash, C. (2022, February 1). *What is self-reflection & how to reflect.* Thriveworks. https://thriveworks.com/blog/importance-self-reflec tion-improvement

Hailey, L. (2022, May 3). *Outgrowing friends? 6 signs you've outgrown your friendship.* Science of People. https://www.scienceofpeople.com/ outgrowing-friends

Harris, A. (n.d.). *10 steps of radical acceptance.* Hopeway. https://hope way.org/blog/radical-acceptance

Harris, M. (2021, June 21). *How to decompress after experiencing a grief trigger.* Mekelharrisphd.Com. https://mekelharrisphd.com/2021/ 06/21/how-to-decompress-after-experiencing-a-grief-trigger

Heinzerling, K. (2022, September 6). *What is ketamine therapy?* Pacific Neuroscience Institute. https://www.pacificneuroscienceinstitute. org/blog/trip/what-is-ketamine-therapy

Helbert, K. (2011, June 27). *Creating rituals to move through grief.* Goodtherapy. https://www.goodtherapy.org/blog/creating-rituals-to-move-through-grief

Herbet-Smith, K. (n.d.). *The importance of self-reflection.* Iris Connect. https://blog.irisconnect.com/uk/community/blog/importance-of-self-reflection/

Hicking, S. (2022, January 4). *Children four times more likely to take up smoking if their parents are smokers.* NHE. https://www.national healthexecutive.com/articles/children-more-likely-to-smoke-if-their-parents-are-smokers

Hill, D. (2017, April 5). *20 simple ways to bring positive energy into life right now.* Lifehack. https://www.lifehack.org/569466/how-regain-your-positive-energy-when-things-are-getting-tough

Honest | etymology, origin and meaning of honest by etymonline. (n.d.). https://www.etymonline.com/word/honest

Horsley, G. (2021, October 6). *How to honor someone after loss.* Forbes.

https://www.forbes.com/sites/forbesnonprofitcouncil/2021/10/06/how-to-honor-someone-after-loss

How can music affect your mood and reduce stress? (2021, April 19). Psychreg. https://www.psychreg.org/music-affect-mood-reduce-stress

How the benefits of sauna can improve mood & mental health. (2022, October 21). Sauna House. https://www.saunahouse.com/blogs/wellness-guide/how-the-benefits-of-sauna-can-improve-mood-mental-health

Involuntary memory. (2023). Wikipedia. https://en.wikipedia.org/w/index.php?title=Involuntary_memory&oldid=1147034031

Joelving, F. (2009, July 12). *Why the #$%! do we swear? For pain relief.* Scientific American. https://www.scientificamerican.com/article/why-do-we-swear

John Lennon quote. (n.d.). A-Z Quotes. https://www.azquotes.com/quote/494675

JuneHealth. (2020, October 6). *The importance of routines to emotional health.* June Health. https://junehealth.com/articles/the-importance-of-routines-to-emotional-health

Kabir, H. (n.d.). *5 questions to ask yourself to determine what you really want.* Happify.Com. https://www.happify.com/hd/determine-what-you-really-want

Kirby, A. (2022, December 16). *The secret ingredient for taming the pungent taste of onions? Lemon juice!* The Mama Report. https://themamareport.com/the-secret-ingredient-for-taming-the-pungent-taste-of-onions-lemon-juice

Kruger, K. (2015, January 15). *Why slow is the way to go: 6 reasons to take your time.* Tiny Buddha. https://tinybuddha.com/blog/slow-way-go-6-reasons-take-time

Kübler-Ross, E., & Kessler, D. (n.d.). *Five stages of grief.* Grief.Com. https://grief.com/the-five-stages-of-grief

Le Cunff, A. (2021, June 24). *An ode to slowness: The benefits of slowing down.* Ness Labs. https://nesslabs.com/the-benefits-of-slowing-down

Lily Tomlin Quote: "Forgiveness means giving up all hope for a better past."

(n.d.). https://quotefancy.com/quote/64859/Lily-Tomlin-Forgiveness-means-giving-up-all-hope-for-a-better-past

Loebl, R. (2015, August 13). *Trauma, addiction & bipolar disorder: Amy's story*. RCOSF. https://rcosf.com/coping-and-personal-growth/trauma-addiction-bipolar-disorder-amys-story

"Make your bed". (2021, August 3). James Clear. https://jamesclear.com/great-speeches/make-your-bed-by-admiral-william-h-mcraven

McDermott, N. (2022, December 14). *What is radical acceptance?* Forbes Health. https://www.forbes.com/health/mind/what-is-radical-acceptance/

Miller, M. (2018, June 19). *Turning a breakup into a positive experience*. New York Times. https://www.nytimes.com/2018/06/19/smarter-living/turning-a-breakup-into-a-positive-experience.html

Morgan, C. (2023, March 16). *60 must-knows to end a relationship on good terms & not leave it messy*. LovePanky. https://www.lovepanky.com/love-couch/broken-heart/how-to-end-a-relationship-on-good-terms

Morisson, D. (2020, August 7). *How to honor yourself and your life choices*. Purpose Fairy. https://www.purposefairy.com/91281/honor-your self-and-your-life-choices

Mort, A. (2023, January 6). *19 | The deep benefits of slowing down*. Andy Mort. https://www.andymort.com/19-the-deep-benefits-of-slowing-down

Nall, R. (2018, May 25). *What are the benefits of sunlight?* Healthline. https://www.healthline.com/health/depression/benefits-sunlight

Native american culture—Sweat lodges. (2021, July 19). Indian Traders. https://indiantraders.com/blogs/news/native-american-culture-sweat-lodges

Naughtygossip. (2018, November 20). *Snoop dogg thanks himself in Hollywood walk of fame speech*. Naughty Gossip. https://www.naughtygossip.com/wink/snoop-dogg-thanks-himself-in-holly wood-walk-of-fame-speech

Newhouse, L. (2021, March 1). *Is crying good for you?* Harvard Health. https://www.health.harvard.edu/blog/is-crying-good-for-you-2021030122020

Oviir, A. (2019, August 6). *Here's why the history of the sauna is deeper than you might think*. Estonian Saunas Magazine. https://medium. com/estoniansaunas/heres-why-the-history-of-the-sauna-is-deeper-than-you-might-think-d8e5127a8232

Pacey, R. (2021, January 20). *The importance of self-reflection*. Infinite Care. https://www.infin8care.com.au/the-importance-of-self-reflection

Pangilinan, J. (2023, June 13). *51 healing quotes for rejuvenating body & mind*. Happier Human. https://www.happierhuman.com/quotes-about-healing

Perina, K. (2016, May 16). *The power of positive self-talk*. Psychology Today. https://www.psychologytoday.com/us/blog/hope-relation ships/201605/the-power-positive-self-talk

Perry, E. (2023, February 21). *Let go and move on: 15 tips to forget the past*. BetterUp.Com. https://www.betterup.com/blog/how-to-forget-the-past

Personal growth through self-reflection. (2021, July 9). Best Day Psychiatry & Counseling. https://bestdaypsych.com/personal-growth-through-self-reflection

Pestana, C. (2022, May 31). *5 grief rituals to help you process & acknowledge loss*. Cake Blog. https://www.joincake.com/blog/grief-rituals

Peterson, R. (2021, September 20). *Coping with sentimental objects after loss*. Medium. https://griefrefuge.medium.com/coping-with-senti mental-objects-after-loss-a0625fa9b6c8

Postle, L. (n.d.). *Grief triggers—should we avoid or embrace them?* GriefAndSympathy.Com. https://www.griefandsympathy.com/grief-triggers.html

Radical acceptance coping mantras. (n.d.). Positive Psychology. https:// positive.b-cdn.net/wp-content/uploads/2020/10/Radical-Acceptance-Coping-Mantras.pdf

Radical acceptance worksheet. (n.d.). Positive Psychology. https://positive. b-cdn.net/wp-content/uploads/Radical-Acceptance-Worksheet.pdf

Raypole, C. (2020, November 23). *Guilt Makes a Heavy Burden. Don't Let It Drag You Down*. Healthline. https://www.healthline.com/health/mental-health/how-to-stop-feeling-guilty

Rebecca. (2022, January 26). *17 simple ways to make peace with yourself.*

Minimalism Made Simple. https://www.minimalismmadesimple.com/home/make-peace-with-yourself

Richards, L. (2022, March 18). *What is positive self-talk?* https://www.medicalnewstoday.com/articles/positive-self-talk

Santos-Longhurst, A. (2018, September 14). *Everything You Need to Know about Sensory Deprivation Tank Therapy.* Healthline. https://www.healthline.com/health/sensory-deprivation-tank

Scott, E. (2022, November 7). *What is the law of attraction? How your thoughts can influence outcomes in your life.* Verywell Mind. https://www.verywellmind.com/understanding-and-using-the-law-of-attraction-3144808

Setting radical acceptance goals. (n.d.). Positive Psychology. https://positive.b-cdn.net/wp-content/uploads/2020/10/Setting-Radical-Acceptance-Goals.pdf

Shada, J. (2022, August 12). *The American dream (or nightmare).* https://www.linkedin.com/pulse/american-dream-nightmare-jeff-shada-mba

Sharma, R., & Akingbule, N. (2018, August 16). *What to do when all your favourite foods remind you of your ex.* Vice. https://www.vice.com/en/article/ev8qbw/what-to-do-when-all-your-favourite-foods-remind-you-of-your-ex

Sharma, S. (2023, February 25). *8 subtle ways to honor yourself (and why you should).* Calm Sage. https://www.calmsage.com/ways-to-honor-yourself

Smith, C. (2021, October 1). *Recognizing grief trigger warnings.* Psychology Today. https://www.psychologytoday.com/us/blog/writing-between-the-lines/202110/recognizing-grief-trigger-warnings

Spadaro, P. (2016, September 28). *How to Honor Yourself: 10 Powerful Ways to Make Yourself a Priority.* Complete Wellbeing. https://completewellbeing.com/article/10-ways-honour/

Stearn, E. (2020, November 11). *How to deal with memories after a breakup.* Forgetting Fairytales. https://www.forgettingfairytales.com/memories-after-a-breakup

Stinson, A. (2018, June 1). *Box breathing: How to do it, benefits, and tips.*

Medical News Today https://www.medicalnewstoday.com/articles/321805

Swaim, E. (2022, May 28). *8 health benefits of getting back to nature and spending time outside*. Healthline. https://www.healthline.com/health/health-benefits-of-being-outdoors

Sweatt, L. (2021, March 3). *17 quotes about finding inner peace*. SUCCESS. https://www.success.com/17-quotes-about-finding-inner-peace/

"The best way out is always through." (Robert Frost). (2019, April 16). Quotation Celebration. https://quotationcelebration.wordpress.com/2019/04/15/the-best-way-out-is-always-through-robert-frost/

These are the 5 ways to implement a new routine in your life. (n.d.). Holmes Place. https://www.holmesplace.com/en/en/blog/lifestyle/5-ways-implement-new-routine-life

Tinsley, A. (2020, April 14). *The mental and emotional benefits of exercise*. True Fitness. https://truefitness.com/resources/mental-emotional-benefits-exercise

Torgovnick May, K. (2012, October 1). *Some examples of how power posing can actually boost your confidence*. TED Blog. https://blog.ted.com/10-examples-of-how-power-posing-can-work-to-boost-your-confidence

Vincenty, S. (2020, November 20). *How to Find Inner Peace and Happiness in the Chaos*. Oprah Daily. https://www.oprahdaily.com/life/a29474453/how-to-find-inner-peace

Watson, K. (2020, October 26). *What is a sound bath? Everything you need to know*. Healthline. https://www.healthline.com/health/sound-bath

What is Positive Self-Talk: 21 Examples of Positive Self-Talk Statements. (n.d.). Miss Tea Positive. https://www.missteapositive.com/blog/examples-of-positive-self-talk-to-practice-positive-self-talk

Why, when, and how to start cutting people out of your life. (2023, March 30). Regain. https://www.regain.us/advice/general/why-when-and-how-to-start-cutting-people-out-of-your-life

Wolfelt, A. (2014, March 21). *Why rituals help us mourn...and heal*. Taps. https://www.taps.org/articles/20-1/rituals

Wu, C. (2019, April 29.). *Good grief: Honoring relationships ending* (70). Embody Your Nature. https://candicewu.com/good-grief-honoring-relationships-ending

You Get What You Put Out Into The World. (n.d.). Wanderlust Worker. https://www.wanderlustworker.com/you-get-what-you-put-out-into-the-world

Zeel. (2022, September 12). *Massage: The natural solution for mental health.* Zeel. https://www.zeel.com/blog/mental-health/research-backed-reasons-you-need-a-massage-for-your-mental-health

www.ingramcontent.com/pod-product-compliance
Lightning Source LLC
Chambersburg PA
CBHW071323150726
47997CB00002B/585